A TREASURY OF EARLY AMERICAN HOMES

A Treasury of

EARLY AMERICAN HOMES

by RICHARD PRATT

Whittlesey House

McGRAW-HILL BOOK COMPANY, INC. · NEW YORK · LONDON · TORONTO

A TREASURY OF EARLY AMERICAN HOMES

PUBLISHED BY WHITTLESEY HOUSE

A division of the McGraw-Hill Book Company, Inc.

PRINTED IN THE UNITED STATES OF AMERICA

FOREWORD

THIS book was made possible by the previous publication in the *Ladies' Home Journal* of the twenty-two color-illustrated articles now brought together here between covers. For it would appear that only a magazine with millions of readers is able to undertake a project whose preparation costs alone—of research, travel, photography, and color engravings —would make this kind of a book by itself prohibitive in price. . . . So thanks to the *Journal's* editors, Bruce and Beatrice Blackmar Gould, who first put forth the idea of the Regional Series and then gave the book idea their backing, and to The Curtis Publishing Company, which freely donated the indispensable printing plates, we have "A Treasury of Early American Homes."

As the Goulds have previously written, "Here in this country, instead of palaces, temples, tombs, or cathedrals, the real historical monuments are the fine old homes that tell the history of our American people. They keep a personal and appealing record of the way people lived when the nation was young.

"The fascination they still have for people today is clearly shown by the large and ever increasing number of yearly visitors to well-preserved places like Charleston and Natchez; to the almost untouched tidewater sections of Virginia and Maryland, where organized pilgrimages are made every spring; and to restorations like that most remarkable one at Williamsburg. Also, by the enthusiastic way the Regional Series, brought together in this book, has been received by readers of the *Ladies' Home Journal.*

"Perhaps a thousand exemplars of these fine old houses still survive, along with many minor examples, out of ten times as many in which people once lived and made our history. Fire, storm, and war have done much of the devastating. Periods of poverty and neglect have destroyed others. But the ones remaining indicate that the houses which have disappeared might still be standing if it were simply a question of their original strength and durability. They were built to last.

"This new interest in our heritage homes is a hopeful sign that the houses which are left will be encouraged to keep on living as beautifully as they appear in these pages."

An attempt has been made to place the houses here in historical sequence, separating them at the same time into three major sections like scenes in a play. All of which I hope will meet with the approval of any expert in the audience, who I am sure will be the first to see that the performance here has been planned not only for enlightenment but for entertainment in particular. And I think it is safe to say that as far as this visual pleasure is concerned, no book has ever before even begun to depict our country's early golden age of houses so effectively and faithfully in color. By that token, its intention, whatever it may teach, is clearly one of pure enjoyment.

I feel that I can speak this way because in a sense it was merely my good fortune to be on hand at the opportunity of a lifetime. It was like being let into a fabulous cavern of treasures from which I was enabled to emerge, month after month, with my arms as full as I could hold them. . . . What was it like? The question came up in various ways. How did we find all these houses in the first place? How did we get permission to use them after we had found them? And how did we go about photographing them?

Although I have spent most of my life scrutinizing houses, old and new, the search for and the selection of many houses here turned out to be more of a task than I'd expected. For the problem was not simply to get together the great houses and the good houses of the past, but to get them *looking* great and good. And sad to say, many remaining originals of once rare distinction are now ruins of neglect, disaster, and regrettable alterations. Time after time I have at last come face to face with a once beautiful old house only to find it either pitifully down-at-heels, wretchedly remodeled, or furnished completely out of character. Happily, however, the book bears witness to countless houses that have never looked better in their lives.

Quite a few of the houses were old acquaintances when the work began; others I already knew by reputation, and some turned up in searches among past periodicals, pictures, and books (see the Bibliography, page 134). Suggestions from friends and readers were frequently most fruitful; and the rest came to light in the course of looking over localities famous for their early architecture. You could never be altogether sure; but a clue was a clue, and you tracked it down, by plane, train, car, and occasionally on foot. And sometimes your breath, which you were holding, was taken away by what you saw.

Permission to photograph and publish had to be obtained rather delicately at times. For one thing, you could never be certain until you had looked a house over, inside and out, whether it was going to be suitable for pictures. It was only polite to let people know you were coming, and only fair to tell them that the first visit was frankly exploratory. A few owners were disinclined even to let me take a look, and while I could never quite see eye to eye with them on their reasons for this attitude, I could at least remind myself how I might feel if someone were to drive up to my door on a similar errand. In the case of a house I was eager to use, it was ordinarily enough, when faced with refusal, to point out the pleasure that millions of people all over the country would miss. As it turned out, I am glad to say that every house I tried to get is now safely in the book.

Reluctance lessened, of course, as the series progressed, and people became familiar with the kind of presentation we were making. But reluctance was never the rule; quite the opposite. In the case of houses now open to the public as living museums we were welcomed with open arms. At the Whipple house; the Wythe; the Hammond-Harwood and the mansions in Fairmount Park; the Tapping-Reeve; Monticello; the Peirce-Nichols and the Pingree, the people in charge couldn't have been more cordial: they put the keys in our hands, placed themselves at our disposal, and made the privilege in every way a pleasure.

When it came to the houses that were privately owned, the privilege was perhaps even greater for its being of a more personal nature. For photographing rooms in color can play hob with the habits of the household. But if I ever detected a sign of impatience on the part of an owner, even of one who was reluctant to start, it escapes me now.

In any event, after arrangements had been made, a station wagon would drive up, loaded to the roof, and a photographer and his assistant would begin discharging huge cases of equipment at the door. Another car or two would arrive containing sundry helpers, me, and boxes of flowers. And I hasten to insert that on many occasions especially valuable assistance contributing to the pictures' full effectiveness was furnished by my wife. Her advice was sound, her eye quick to catch the easily overlooked details, her feminine first aid invaluable in quite a few emergencies. When she was there, time counted for twice as much, in every way.

At any rate, here we were; and while cameras, floodlights, and cables were being unpacked and put together, while a technical assistant with a torch was locating electric connections in the cellar, and cartons of flowers were being uncovered,

the camera angles were studied, room by room, and scheduled to catch the sunlight as it moved around from window to window. Then, with picture positions planned, floodlights were maneuvered into place and the first room would be readied for its most becoming pose.

Without going into more of these details than might add interest to the pictures that follow, it is enough to say that in rearranging any given area the purpose was always to bring out the flavor and personality of the room as faithfully as possible, giving to the fixed stare of the camera the final effect of a roving eye. In quite a few cases this meant moving furniture, rugs, pictures; taking some pieces out entirely, and now and then substituting articles from other parts of the house. Owners who allowed themselves to witness the operation often winced, but under the spell of the floodlights and in the general confusion of cables, cameras, and panting personnel, they assumed, outwardly at least, an attitude of calm toward what must have seemed to them at times rather ruthless activities on our part, falling in, almost always, with the spirit of the proceedings. In fact, there was more than one instance when, after the picture was taken, rather than let us return the room to its original state, they would ask us to leave everything as we'd fixed it for the photograph—liked it better that way.

During these goings on indoors, I would keep one eye on the sunlight outside, and when the light was right I would tear myself away and take up my own camera to get pictures of the house or the town. This was perhaps a selfish intrusion into the province of the professional cameraman; but it was a temptation I couldn't resist. Nor could anyone else, I am sure, have resisted it who ever had a chance to place his head under a focusing cloth and see the glowing images of these unforgettable houses and their glamorous settings on the ground glass of a big eight-by-ten.

Weather was our worst enemy, but most of the time we were extremely lucky. The essential thing was sunlight, and if it wasn't there, we simply had to wait for it—which, in a place like New Orleans, where it rained for days, was no particular hardship. Summertime, in general, had certain disadvantages. The heaviness of the foliage could not only obscure the house from without but rob us of the indoor sunlight that we counted on to give the rooms a lively sparkle. In winter owners were often away and the house was closed up; the scene outside was apt to be bleak; and while a setting in the snow was something we always hoped to get, we were never able to time it right, which is why this one picturesque aspect fails to appear.

With a few exceptions, all our pictures were therefore taken in the spring and fall. Then, either the early buds were breaking, or the foliage was thinning out and turning on its autumn tints; the grass was green, there were flowers in bloom, and the sunlight was soft and slanting. Though I wonder now why we were so concerned about surrounding effects—the houses were sufficiently wonderful by themselves, regardless.

RICHARD PRATT

CONTENTS

historical building methods and fashions funneled through what was then held by most Americans to be the Mother Country. And by glancing back at the panorama of our past, which these houses adorn so handsomely, we can see how in their new environment all these homes of English breeding took on in time a character that became as American as the people who put them up and occupied them. The New Englanders remembered the humble Elizabethan cottages of the southeastern counties they had left behind; the new Virginians the larger and lesser houses nearer London. And those were quite accountably the homes they chose to emulate here throughout the formative years of the Colonies. They built from memory, and their memory was good, as anyone will agree who compares the surviving seventeenth-century houses of New England with the village architecture of Essex and Cambridgeshire, Surrey and Kent. Witness the Whipple house in the Ipswich chapter, whose prototype, for all I know, may still be standing somewhere back in Middlesex. And the same, with variations, holds true of the much smaller handful of existing seventeenth-century houses from Philadelphia south.

In several ways, however, it was impossible for the early colonists to translate literally from the architecture of the homeland, especially in New England, where the climate required more protection against both cold and heat than was needed in the more moderate seasons of southeastern England. Besides, here there was lumber galore, with which to board the walls against the weather. For while weatherboarding was by no means unknown in England, it was customary there to leave the framing timbers of the house exposed, filled between with brick and plaster; a style of structure that was at first tried here—and found wanting. Much, much later,—after 1850 and therefore beyond the scope and purpose of this present book—a half-timber craze did hit us hard. But that was a skin-deep style; had nothing to do with structure; had to do only with the romantic era, as of this moment just coming to a timely close, as many moderns hope. This half-timber madness, like many romantic fashions from 1850 to now, was a false face on the framing of a house; whereas in the seventeenth-century Colonies structure was something too vital to toy with. There were reasons of life and death why it had to be honest and right.

So for altogether functional reasons the early New England Colonists covered their cottages with clapboard and built enormous chimneys out of all traditional proportion to the size of the house, just as their fellow Colonists were doing further south. They made their windows smaller; not merely to help keep out the northern cold, but partly for the same reason that they whittled their hardware out of hickory and used pegs instead of nails; which was because of a fantastic tax on window glass and metalware, imposed by the Crown, like the tax on tea. But it was less obnoxious in the end, for soon, under cover, the Colonists began to make nails and locks and glass for themselves. They couldn't grow their own tea, but they could build their own houses, and their houses grew more and more American as the seventeenth century came to an end.

Elizabethan English was the flavor still, but the form and

feel, the texture, the whole new look, were creating an architecture that was getting ready to declare its independence. You can call it Early Colonial. As an American style, loosely entitled the Cape Cod Cottage, its popularity has persisted, with few interruptions, right through to the present; living now primarily on what is left of its style alone and on the sentiment, surrounding it, of home, sweet home.

In the meanwhile, a new style was gaining ground in England. And because of the Kings in whose reigns it developed, it was known as Georgian. It was introduced from Renaissance Italy by Inigo Jones, and this famous English exponent of academic formality in architecture caused a fashion for pure form to supersede the medieval manner of building—a manner which had found its way here, as we have seen, to give our early Colonial houses their truly functional quality. Whereas the Renaissance style inaugurated in London by the celebrated Jones was another dish, decidedly; and as the houses in the second part of this book disclose, it was soon to appear on the American table.

But first it was to be adapted over there to something less monumental than palaces, public buildings, and vast country places. And in England, in the hands of Sir Christopher Wren, it became in that process one of the most gracious and becoming fashions ever applied to building, from manor houses down to modest dwellings. Its burst into popularity came at a most propitious time, following the great Fire of London; for on the face of the phoenix that rose from London's ashes the features were definitely and handsomely Georgian. And it wasn't long before those features became familiar in American façades.

Georgian came ashore at Williamsburg and spread up the James, as you will see from the pictures of Westover, the Wythe House, Carter's Grove, and Berkeley. It laid its loveliness on Charleston, Alexandria, New Castle, Philadelphia. It covered the Colonies with glory, especially where wealth and culture could give it their blessing. But though the responsibility was Wren's in a way, that architect never came in person to this country as has been rumored, nor was he ever the architect, *in absentia*, of any houses here.

The architects of this new style came here in bundles. They were books from London, inspired by the riches of the English Renaissance and filled with details carefully drawn, which Colonial craftsmen were quick to master. Handbooks for builders, their authors were men to remember and admire—William Halfpenny, Batty Langley, Robert Morris, William Pain, Abraham Swan. Our Later Colonial owes them its deepest debt of gratitude. For more doorways than you can mention, more mantels, windows, cornices, pediments, and paneling came straight from their pages than from any other source.

Many actual English craftsmen came as well, like Richard Bayliss and David Minitree for Carter's Grove, and William Buckland for Gunston Hall on the Potomac, and the Hammond-Harwood House in Annapolis. And of course these men spread the good work while they were here, helping the hands of Colonial carpenters and adapting the new architecture to Colonial towns and countrysides, and to the requirements of

Colonial owners as well. To the point, that, with the hand-books for assistance, almost any able builder could draw up and erect a Georgian house. Men of means and taste became architectural amateurs, and gave their Georgian homes a real American personality, as many of the pictures that follow here make plain.

So that by the time of the Revolution, the country's manners were architecturally mature. For Americans who liked to live the forthright simplicity of Early Colonial, a style of this kind had already been established. For those who preferred formality of plan and appearance, the Georgian style had been developed into a Later Colonial whose roots had taken kindly to our cultural soil. You could take your choice. For every Sandwich there was an Alexandria; for every Whipple house, a Westover.

But just as there can be no accounting for taste, there was no accounting, at this point in history, for the temper of the times; and by the time the Declaration of Independence was signed, the Revolution won, and the nation on its own, a change in both temper and taste was taking place. And it wasn't long before it began to show in our houses, particularly and at first in the homes of intellectuals, and most of all, and soonest, in the home of Thomas Jefferson at Monticello.

Jefferson was the most architecturally conscious statesman in the country—skillful and scholarly, and sternly devoted to the Classical style. That academic devotion had not only an aesthetic basis, but an emotional one as well; and on both scores he was scathing in his denunciation of Georgian design. The architecture of Williamsburg filled him with scorn; its prettiness seemed to him a parody of the only architecture worth while: the noble monuments of Greece and Rome. Emotionally he felt that Greece and Rome, apart from the beauty of their buildings, had much in common with our new United States; for they too, in their prime, had been young republics. And as a leader of this young republic here, a man of extraordinary parts and power, he was able to influence taste with great dispatch and wide effect. His own architecture is among the finest in the American past; but even more than examples of his work, like Monticello and the University of Virginia, his compelling passion for the Classical mode was the force that helped to change the tide of American taste.

Other forces were moving concurrently. And perhaps the most important of these were of English origin—bringing us back to that family tree. There was Lord Byron, for one, who with a poet's pervasiveness was making the world aware of the plight of Greece, then under attack by the barbarous Turks. And for another, there were the measured drawings that James Stuart and Nicholas Revett had made of Classical remains in Greece and Italy. These drawings appeared in London—great folios of engravings—adding fuel, as it were, to Byron's flames. That was all that was needed, not only to complete our identification here with those ancient other young republics, but to provide us with the means of reproducing here what seemed in the circumstances a most appropriate style of architecture. And the means of reproducing that architecture were facilitated by the appearance in London, and soon thereafter here, of builders' handbooks once again; but this time putting pure Classicism to work—at least as pure as possible, considering the transition that had to be made from ancient temples to contemporary houses, and from monumental masonry to domestic wood and plaster.

In the hands of Jefferson and a gathering group of able architects, this Classic urge produced a style of undeniable dignity, and in the later work of McIntire in Salem, and other architect-craftsmen elsewhere, it achieved a lush and eloquent beauty. It became for a while, in fact, what many consider the most authentically American manner of building, from mansions like Andalusia to templelike cottages. But as its popularity spread and the manner began to lose whatever meaning it had, the Greek Revival grew quainter and quainter, weaker and weaker. A Gothic revival, to become equally quaint, was coming to life in England; Ruskin was writing, and disciples here were stirring with new ideas. It was nearing 1850, and the Romantic Era was arriving, with an assortment of theatrical styles in which to disguise the Industrial Age. Early Colonial was having a relapse; Georgian was no longer liked; and the Classical Revival was subsiding. For fifty years or more to come, the houses collected here in this book were to be out of fashion, out of favor.

But before it was too late the twentieth century came to the rescue. Memories of our native architecture returned from distant periods of the past to please us once again. We began looking up the old houses, and in turn the old houses themselves began looking up; and as might have been expected, our new houses began looking more or less the way the old ones did in the early days. And while many have been undeniably handsome, nostalgia was not enough; the impulse of the real originals was missing, along with yesterday's necessities.

We have been building on borrowed architecture. Today's necessities, no longer new, are asking with greater and greater urgency for methods, materials, and means of production which rightly belong to the age in which we live today. And a new era in architecture is at last arriving.

Among the things to keep in mind while planning for the future are these houses of our inheritance. Perhaps in part they belong to the past, but in part perhaps to the present, too. At least let us hope that they will always haunt us with their beauty.

Queen Elizabeth (1533–1603)

The Medieval Look

in America

EARLY COLONIAL

Elizabethan Cottage

WHILE the first arrivals here to stay were tacking into coves and inlets up and down the coast, sailing up rivers and bays, with wonder in their eyes, Shakespeare was finishing "The Tempest," St. Peter's was being completed, Milton and Rembrandt were born, and Richelieu was the power behind the throne of France. On the map of America, place names were beginning to appear. Jamestown, Plymouth, Portsmouth, New Amsterdam, Salem, Marblehead, Boston; Dutch names up the Hudson, Scandinavian up the Delaware, and Indian names dotted all directions. Names of people, too, began coming into Colonial prominence: John Smith, Powhatan, and John Rolfe's celebrated bride, the legendary Pocahontas; Governor William Berkeley of Virginia; William Bradford, Myles Standish and William Brewster, of Mayflower fame, along with Endecotts, Carters, Winthrops and Mathers, Stuyvesants and Rensselaers, from Long Island to Albany, Johan Printz and Chief Tishcohan, where Delaware is now; Calverts and Claibornes, in Maryland; Lords Ashley, Berkeley and Craven in Carolina. And most of the names of places and people were English. . . . Things began to appear. By 1633 the first power sawmill was ripping logs into lumber on the Piscataqua. Settlers in 1611 at Jamestown were beginning to make brick, and shortly after, so were the Dutch at

Albany and the Pilgrims in Massachusetts. Colonial glass began to take the place of oil paper for window panes; and tinsmiths and cabinetmakers were making household implements and furniture. The methods were medieval and went with the houses' medieval look.

The first English settlement in America was made at Jamestown four years after the death of England's spinster Queen. But already, to a New World region that was vast and vague, Elizabeth had given the name Virginia, thus commemorating the peculiar nature of her Royal person. To the period of her lengthy reign her name at home had been attached by bonds that never can be broken as long as language lives. And in the Elizabethan tradition lie not only the finest of poetry, but a method and manner of homebuilding whose effects will be felt as long as people live in houses. Very clearly, this effect can be felt in the houses that follow immediately in this first section of the book. These take in parts of three separate centuries: late seventeenth and eighteenth in New England; early nineteenth in Pennsylvania. All derive their functional form from a medieval manner and method of building which can today be found in the best of our contemporary domestic modern—a far cry now from those wilderness days and wilderness conditions that witnessed our earliest attempts at architecture.

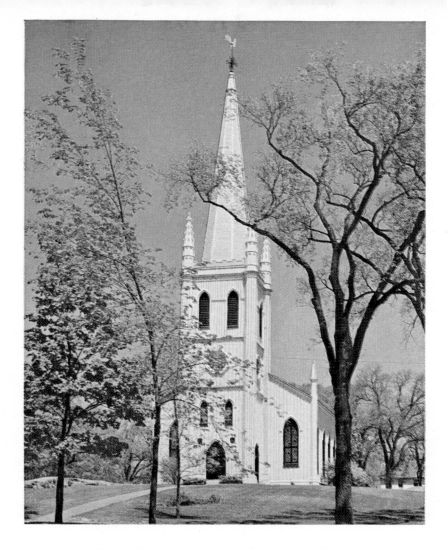

North Church, an early example of wooden Gothic.

IPSWICH, MASS.

FOR seventeenth-century houses you can hardly do better than Ipswich—it being the claim of this charming old Massachusetts place that within the town itself, and along its outlying lanes, there are more of our earliest homes than anywhere else in the land. Not only do the houses send you back three hundred years to the time of the town's original settlers, but the Ipswich telephone book today gives you the names of those earliest families—descendants of a long line of local citizens whose enduring devotion to the place is of course the secret of the well-preserved appearance that Ipswich now presents. There may be slightly older houses elsewhere, but nowhere, to my knowledge, a more complete assembly of this pioneer period.

Every summer, in July, they celebrate a Seventeenth Century Day, and open all the historical homes to the public. But next to being there on that occasion, these six pages of pictures will give you the best idea it is possible to get of the beauty that was built into these first American houses. Their roots of style and structure stem from Elizabethan cottages of Southeastern England, from where the Pilgrims came; but here, in Massachusetts, because of a more rigorous climate and unlimited lumber, they took on at once a new American look. In them was born, thereby, a method and manner of building which is still going strong three centuries later, from here to every corner of the country coast to coast.

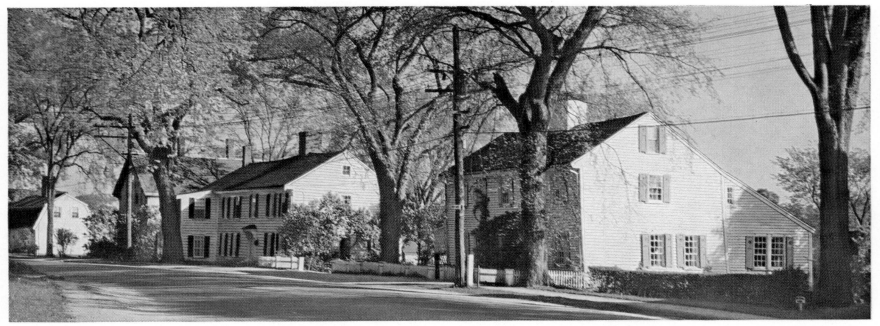

Ipswich River (facing page) rises and falls with the tide, through the town, bordered by ancient dwellings like the 1648 Emerson House that faces the old stone bridge.

Under the elms of High Street are the 1680 "House with the Orange Shutters," the Kimball House, built in 1715, and the gambrel-roofed Fowler House, 1720.

"Overhang" construction of east side of Whipple House and diamond-paned windows show colonists' liking for Elizabethan traditions.

This room was added as a kitchen in 1670. Early American ladder-back chairs face the widespread fireplace with its customary accouterments.

WHIPPLE HOUSE

THIS is without any question one of the very first houses to have been built in the English-speaking colonies of America, still standing today; the Ipswich chronicles setting forth that as early as 1638, a century and a half before the Revolution was won, John Fawn, a Pilgrim settler, began construction on this site. It might even now be known as the Fawn house, had Fawn unfortunately not sold his property within a couple of years. But it was bought and brought to completion by John Whipple, whose name it bears, and whose family and descendants occupied it for the next two centuries; at that, not a record for Ipswich, where another family, the Goodales, still live in the house their forebears built *three* centuries ago. At any rate, for reasons of age and quality, the Whipple House must be reckoned one of the most important in the country; being now preserved as a museum by the Ipswich Historical Society, which has furnished it with many fascinating pieces of the early period, and maintains it with meticulous care. Under those circumstances it should be standing for centuries to come; for after one look inside you can see that it was built to last. Its post-and-beam construction has grown even more solid and secure than it was when first put together; while this hardwood framing, dominated by the tremendous "summer" that supports the ceiling joists, gives the rooms an air of medieval strength and permanence. The roof and weatherboarding may have to undergo minor repairs every half century or so, but the essential body of the house is good enough to last forever.

From its position on the northeast corner of the Village Green where the local militia trained for King Philip's War one hundred years before the American Revolution, this old house has seen the march of many men playing their parts in succeeding chapters of American history. Few houses have witnessed so much, and fewer still look so well today anywhere.

The woodwork of the bedroom is the earliest in the house. Eighteenth-century field bed, with fish-net canopy, has a cross-and-crown coverlet woven in 1750.

LANGDON WARNER

Exterior is distinguished by a salt-box profile, with a hewn overhang on three sides.

CURIOUSLY enough, this house on the outskirts of town, overlooking the meadows that run down to the dunes and the ocean, is not a native of Ipswich, but was brought here about thirty years ago from Newburyport, ten miles away. In its present foster location, where the passage of time seems almost imperceptible, it has found a home where its future is assured; partly because of its present owner, Dr. Langdon Warner, Professor of Oriental Art at Harvard, whose occasional Korean pieces blend beautifully into the early American setting.

The stairway in the entrance hall is one of the most outstanding features of this house, illustrating the transition between the completely enclosed early types and the open, more decorative examples that followed later on.

The original stairway is one of the finest and best-preserved late Seventeenth-century types. English, Oriental and Early American furniture blend harmoniously in the large, heavily beamed living room.

Originally, this long room at the rear of the house was divided into three rooms, with the kitchen occupying the middle section—bedroom and storeroom at either end.

DODGE HOUSE

ACCORDING to Ipswich history, this house was built as a wedding present for the Robert Paine, Jr., who was later to become an important figure in the witchcraft trials at Salem, thirty miles toward Boston from here. The young man had been graduated from Harvard just four years before—in the class of 1656!—and the house into which he moved at his marriage must have been one of the best in the neighborhood, now a few minutes' drive from the center of town. The excellent restoration was accomplished by the late Mrs. Robert Dodge, whose son is now the owner.

A welcome wedding present three centuries ago, or today, you will agree.

The bedroom contains a Sheraton four-poster and Early American hooked rugs.

CONNECTICUT SALT BOX

Nestling back in from the coast line of Connecticut, and on all the way to Cape Cod, you will find the remnants and relics of these wonderful old houses from the 1600's; and occasionally, like this one here, an example so well preserved that it brings that far-off past right up to the present. You can be sure it is not the fault of the house when you find one in ruins, for only neglect and disaster have ever been able to damage or destroy them. The heavy oak with which they were framed has taken on the enduring strength of steel, and the massive single chimneys which furnish great open fireplaces for every room, upstairs and down, are built like the pyramids. Simple to the point of severity, these houses come by their beauty through honest construction.

The typical rear roof line of the 1690 Ogden house at Fairfield, like an old-fashioned salt container, gives these houses their name. The present living room was once the lean-to kitchen, its huge fireplace—center of domestic life—filled with cooking implements. Note the hand-hewn beams after 2½ centuries.

The bed in the principal bedroom is covered with a spread of linsey-woolsey—a homespun, colored with butternut dye. Early primitives decorate the walls, and a Chippendale child's chair stands by the fire.

During the Revolution, when the British landed at Fairfield and burned most of the town, the Ogden house escaped destruction probably because it was off the line of march to Danbury—the invaders' next objective.

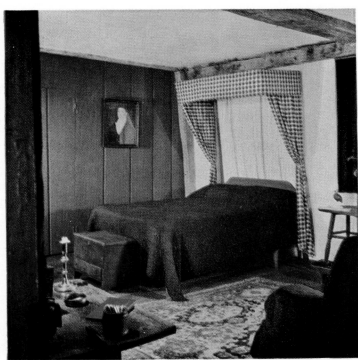

The smaller bedroom, with its little canopy and bed chest, is also completely decorated with homespun fabrics. . . . The Ogden house is now in the fortunate possession of Miss Mary Allis.

The dining room contains many splendid examples of early American furniture, including the gate-leg table and the 1690 banister chairs against the wall. The principal items of furniture in this house date prior to 1750, and all retain their original finish.

Sandwich, Mass.

PICTURESQUE PREFACE TO OLD CAPE COD

THIS village, which lies half hidden off the main highway that hurries along past the elbow of the Cape, and on to Provincetown at the finger tip, is like a page torn out of the past—still clear, clean, fresh and beautiful. The native architecture that it shares with the rest of the Cape, but for which it provides a setting especially choice, is of course the most widely copied in the country. For every town in every state is familiar with various versions of the Cape Cod cottages that were built beside the curving lanes of Sandwich more than two hundred years ago—the imitations never quite matching the fine originals with which this town is filled. The sincerest form of flattery has likewise been heaped upon a special handiwork of this unassuming village— a handiwork as fragile as the houses were strong; for the glassware which originated here in the last century is now imitated far and wide, in vaster quantities than any other

glassware in the world. Elsewhere you can see Sandwich glass and houses of the Sandwich type, but here where they belong you can see them at their best.

The town clusters around the old mill pond in the picture below, then thins out through surrounding cranberry bogs and meadows over to the dunes that guard the Bay. The first permanent settlement on Cape Cod, its boundaries were established three hundred years ago by two no less legendary figures than Capt. Myles Standish and his assistant, John Alden. Daniel Webster was an habitué of the inn up the street which bears his name; and one of the first glass blowers brought from Europe to Sandwich was suspected of being the lost Dauphin of France. And on a quiet solitary morning there, it is easy to imagine that any one of those old characters might still be around, peering out of a window from behind a fabulous piece of Opalescent, Jade Green or Golden Ruby glass.

14

EXTERIOR PHOTOGRAPHS BY RICHARD PRATT. INTERIOR PHOTOGRAPHS BY HAROLD FOWLER.

The rare bowed roofs are framed like the ribs of ships.

One of the very earliest, this house has never been restored.

An original of familiar design, just over in Barnstable.

An unusual example of the two-story "three quarter" type.

15

This "Captain's house" is now owned by Mrs. Charles D. Cook.

The paneled living room was originally the kitchen.

More than two centuries old, this house still keeps its strength and beauty

SANDWICH houses range in size from the tiny "one-quarter Capes" to what might be called the "full-Capes" or "Captain's houses"—like this one that stands on one of the highest knolls of the town. "Half-a-Capes" were houses two windows wide, with a chimney at the end; the owner always hoping the day would come when he could add the other half and convert his cottage into a proper house with a central chimney, such as this, which was built in 1730 as it stands today, commanding a view of the town—a monument to the skill of those early carpenters who framed their wooden houses, regardless of size, for the centuries.

16

Sparkling with priceless Sandwich lamps and vases, Mrs. Cook's sitting room has a remarkable Goddard chest of 1770, and early paper in reproduction.

The dining-room chairs are eighteenth-century Hepplewhite by Goddard of Newport. The glass, quite naturally, is Sandwich.

The guest bedroom, with its inside shutters, has early maple four-posters, hooked rugs, Windsor chairs and more Sandwich glass.

PRATT

Unlike it at first glance, the house of Peter Place Cook is almost identical with that of his mother across the street.

The paneled bedroom meets up with modern paper.

Pointing up the purity of the fireplace wall.

QUAIL HOLLOW, BUILT BY THOMAS TOBEY IN 1724, IS STILL ONE OF THE MOST COLORFUL OF SANDWICH HOUSES.

ONE of the things you notice about the Cape Cod houses of Sandwich is the variety of colors they can wear. Even when paint has never been present on the shingled sides, years of weathering have placed most becoming natural pigments on the cedar, which paint manufacturers have now been able to simulate. And while the walls of most of the painted ones are white, with trim of green, steel blue or gray, others are painted red, pale green, gray, or yellow—like Quail Hollow here.

Nor is severity the rule inside. Many of the floors are gaily spattered with paint drops of green, red, yellow, blue. The walls are often brightly papered, as you can see, and even the unpainted paneling has a special brilliance of its own. And for all their purity and primness within—or perhaps because of it—the Sandwich houses accept gracefully the wisely chosen furnishing and decoration of almost any modest manner from contemporary back to the simple and forthright things which first occupied them when they were new.

The living-room paneling was discovered under old handmade laths, plaster and wallpaper; needing only cleaning and rubbing.

An unusually handsome heirloom piano fits nicely into this parlor, with its Terry clock and Staffordshire hunting figures.

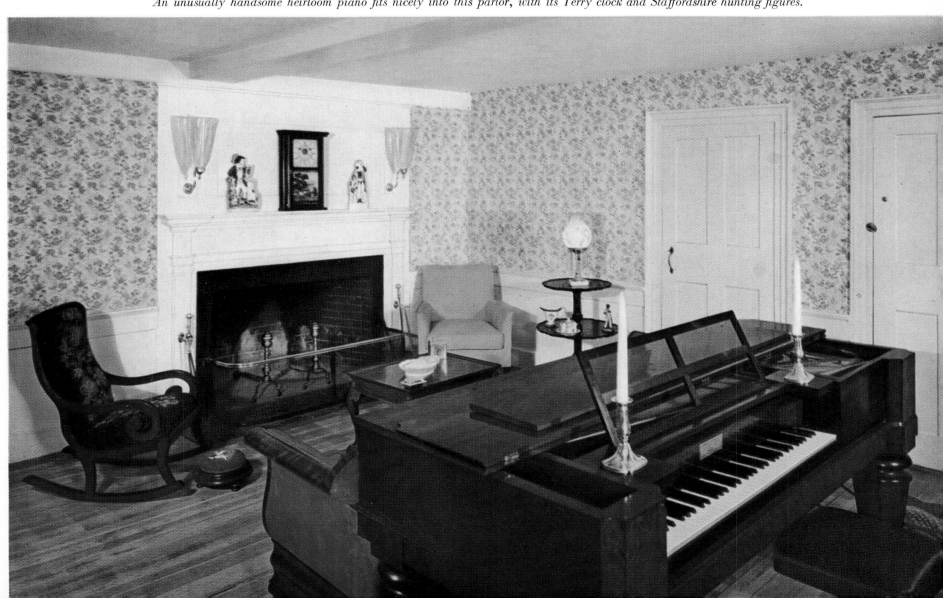

BUCKS COUNTY
Pennsylvania

A land of rich farms and sturdy houses.

COUNTY LINE · *An unusually fine example of the white-plastered Pennsylvania stone house, this one has four distinct roof levels in line, in all likelihood denoting different stages of construction. Note fine rooster weathervane.*

PLEASANT VALLEY · *Buildings like this old farmhouse in the upper part of the county, recently restored, and like its magnificent masonry barn beyond, were all constructed of the stone from their immediate vicinity.*

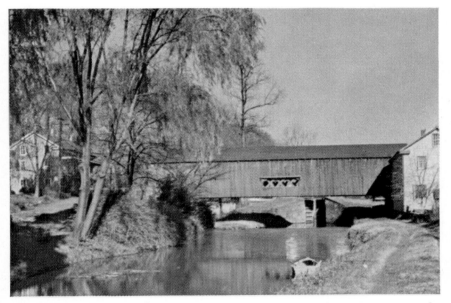

UHLERSTOWN · *Up until twenty years ago, hundreds of barges a month, pulled by mules, passed under this bridge and through the lock beyond, and hamlets like Uhlerstown were leisurely ports of call, with inn and piers.*

UPPER TINICUM · *Now showing signs of occupation by settlers from the city, this plain white farmhouse, like many in its neighborhood, was plastered so as to keep the rain from seeping through its porous stone walls.*

BUCKINGHAM · *Only a Bucks County stone house could take the Victorian period in its stride, and wear so well an 1860 cornice above its 1790 walls, keeping its essential character intact. This one was restored recently.*

SPRINGFIELD · *The farther up the county you go, the more red barns you meet (and green and yellow too); the witch signs decorating their sides to ward off lightning, fire and other ill fortune, increase their picturesqueness.*

This mellow old manor house is Bucks County at its best. Built of what the county people call "tailored" stone, carefully cut and laid, its flat-arched windows and doorway, and its flanking wings at lower level, are signs of its pre-Revolutionary period, when stone houses began to replace the log cabins of the locality's earliest settlers. It is about a mile from New Hope and the Delaware, on the road to Doylestown, and in the section now most heavily resettled by many well-known newcomers from Broadway, Park Avenue and Wall Street, northeast some sixty miles—a geographical fact made hard to believe by such houses, so faraway-looking in time and place.

AQUETONG . **The walls and wood-**

work of Ingham Manor reflect the finest

features of Bucks County architecture

The great feature of the dining room at Ingham Manor, and a characteristic feature of most Bucks County houses built between 1750 and 1850 (which might be called Bucks County's period), is what they call the "walk-in" fireplace; the wide opening supported by a massive lintel log of oak which is faced by a simply molded mantel. A room such as this would originally have been the kitchen, too, of course, and the winter living room as well; the cooking done above and beside a wood fire on the hearth and in a cavelike oven in the chimney's back wall. The floor of Pennsylvania tiles is typical. and the homespun Swedish table cover is set with country ironstone.

It is altogether possible that the extraordinary pine paneling of the living room at Ingham Manor is the work of the shipwrights who settled along the Delaware in the early days, and who turned their hands to house carpentry when boatbuilding was slow, for it has many of the earmarks of their craftsmanship: its simplicity and robust scale, which match so well the sturdy cabinetwork of the big Pennsylvania Dutch wardrobe. Very appropriate in this somewhat primitive room are the two "country Chippendale" chairs, so called because they follow the famous style in almost rustic fashion. The figures are Pennsylvania "chalk"; the plates, Bucks County slip ware.

PHOTOS BY FOWLER

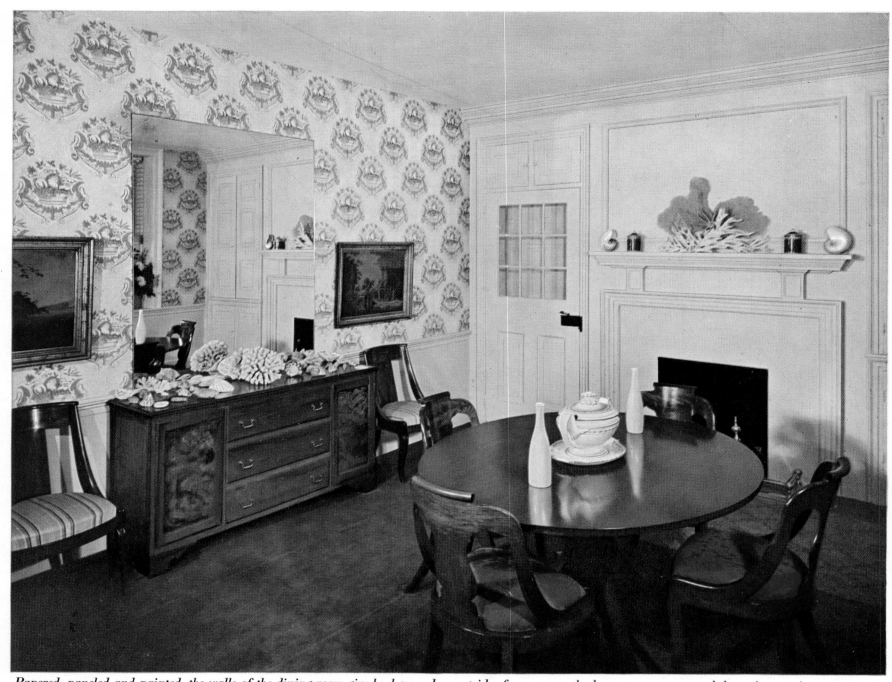

Papered, paneled and painted, the walls of the dining room give background variety to the Empire table, chairs and sideboard, together with an effect of greater size in which the large square sheet of mirror plays its part. While outside, from across the lane, as you can see below, size requires no assistance. The barn has typical Bucks County bigness and beauty, the house it belongs to, a very special stateliness along with its distinguished stonework.

MECHANICSVILLE

· The forthright simplicity of Bucks County interiors provides an ideal background for contemporary color schemes like those shown and for furniture that ranges from Early American to modern.

Here in the high-ceilinged hallway of the Mechanicsville house it takes strap hinges of really prodigious size and strength to carry the weight of the heavy full-height doors, whose whiteness is a wonderful foil to the olive-colored walls.

As you can see by the mantel of the Mechanicsville living room, early Bucks County carpenters had access to handbooks of Georgian details, which, as here, they often simplified. Note how well the room takes to gilt valances and lace.

The guest bedroom is furnished with effective simplicity: Sleigh bed and cloth-draped bedside table, plus two unseen chairs, and chest of drawers. The portrait is a primitive, and by the window are two Pennsylvania Dutch "Fracturs."

SOLEBURY · *Nobody built better in Bucks County than the Quakers, and the meetinghouses of the Friends are models of beautiful masonry and simple, generous proportions, as you can see.*

NEW HOPE · *One of the oldest and most colorful Bucks County towns along the Delaware, long famous for its painters, New Hope's color now is even heightened by its summer-theater atmosphere.*

Sir Christopher Wren (1632–1723)

LATER COLONIAL

The Georgian Look in America

BY 1700 the map of the Colonies was becoming quite noticeably spotted; a few Colonial-size cities, many towns, and hundreds of hamlets; but highways between them were hardly worth marking on the map. And some of the prominent early places had already begun to relinquish their first importance to newer communities nearby—Plymouth to Boston, St. Mary's City to Baltimore, Jamestown to Williamsburg. It was most of all at Williamsburg, Virginia's new Colonial capital, that the new look in architecture which was to give the eighteenth century its predominating flavor here, made its most auspicious bow. And the one big name behind the new style's Colonial debut was that of the architect most responsible for the style's development in England—Sir Christopher Wren. It has been said that certain Williamsburg designs may have come from the drawing board of the master himself, and there are certain buildings in the present Restoration, both reconstructed and original examples, whose appearance would lend weight to this conjecture. In any event, Wren's English work in the Georgian manner was the main aesthetic force behind the best American houses of the time. He had his hands full rebuilding London after the Fire, and his celebrated couplet, "If anyone calls, I'm designing St. Paul's,"

further indicates how much too occupied he must have been at home to take on any Colonial commissions. Fortunately for the quality of our Colonial architecture, however, there were many able artisans who could come over to interpret the style for which he was famous, and a host of builders' handbooks to guide the workmen here, as mentioned in the Introduction to this volume.

It was a century of elegance in Colonial architecture, and a century that saw the ascendancy of figures forever famous in American history—Franklin, Washington, Jefferson. Midway through it, Bach and Handel died, and Voltaire; Mozart and Rousseau lived their lives; Beethoven was born. Colonial culture on the loftier levels reflected the drawing rooms of London and the Continental salons. Colleges were springing up throughout the Colonies. Colonial craftsmen, in metal, glass, and wood, were producing objects, from tableware to furniture, as fine as any from abroad; creating collector's pieces for us to prize in present times. And in the minds of Americans the thought of political independence was taking hold. When it came, the effects were of course profound—on people's lives, our national career, and incidentally on our houses, as the final section will depict.

CHARLESTON

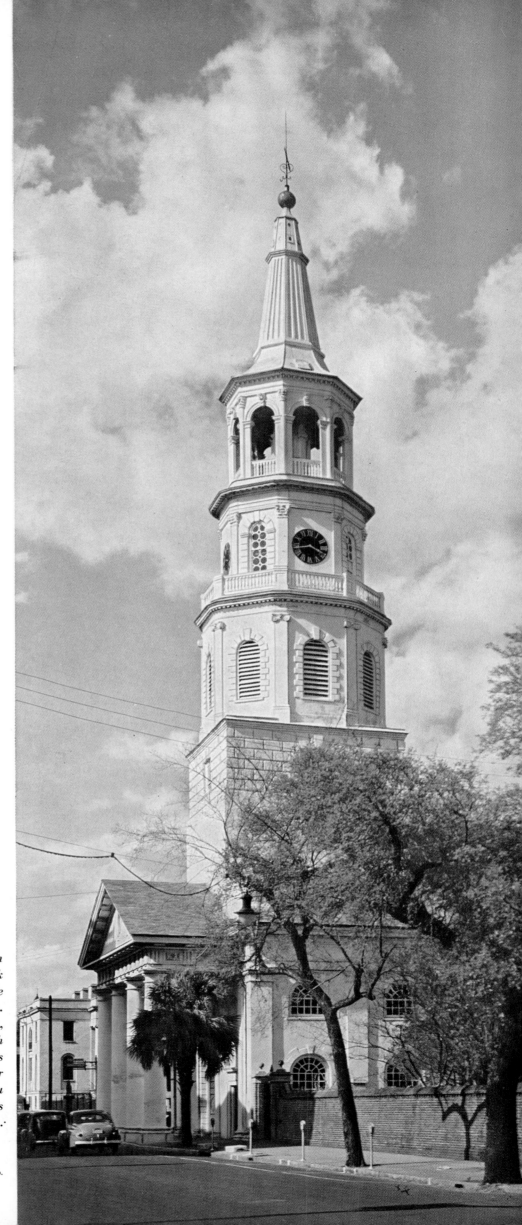

AN even more remarkable thing about old Charleston than her pastel streets, graceful churches, elegant houses and exquisite interiors is the fact than any of these enchantments still remain. For not another Colonial city has suffered such a profusion of calamities, and so many different kinds. Time after time, fire has left great areas of it in ashes, and twice it has been raked by ruinous bombardment—once by the British in the Revolution, and once by Northern cannon in the War Between the States. Then not to be outdone, Nature has forever hurled fierce hurricanes and tornadoes on the town, has even cracked it with more than its quota of earthquakes. Yet now, as you walk through all the large and little streets that lie between South Battery and Broad, and see how richly lined they are with relics of the past, you hardly sense that much of what was there is missing. You only feel that Charleston must lead a charmed life, and a charming one as well.

That charming life is written all over the fine old Charleston houses. To be sure, a lot of the early wealth that produced them has dwindled, and there are places you pass that make this painfully clear. But old-time glories don't give up without a struggle, and the will to keep them alive strikes you as one of Charleston's most endearing qualities, so clearly expressed in her architecture.

This architecture tells the story of a town that already had a cosmopolitan culture two centuries ago—English, French, West Indian. And while there are streets and houses which in turn seem to be more English, more French or more West Indian than others, the final effect is one that belongs right here and nowhere else. The climate, which ranges from temperate to tropical, helped to give all styles a distinctly local character, providing many of the houses, for instance, with their tiers of shadowy piazzas, which protect the rooms within from heat and glare when temperatures are torrid, and make pleasant outdoor sitting rooms in spring and fall, when Charleston weather is wonderful.

Outside Charleston, the famous old plantation houses and fabulous gardens of the Low Country unfold another scene in the same play.

The charm and color of Church Street, on the left, are typical of old Charleston thoroughfares, with house walls of tinted stucco and age-pink brick rising right up from the sidewalk, and with smaller vibrant side streets cutting across, and lush gardens through gateways. The church in the distance in the left-hand picture is St. Philip's, and not to be confused with St. Michael's, which towers up from Meeting Street, one block over, just as it appears on the right. These two Christopher Wren-ish spires punctuate almost every view you get of Charleston, standing above the Old World rooftops and chimney pots to set the style and period of the town.

EXTERIOR PHOTOGRAPHS BY RICHARD PRATT, INTERIOR PHOTOGRAPHS BY BALZ-SELWYN LTD.

The Staats House

This is one of the houses which survived the devastating fire of 1740, and stands on one of the very rare grants of land made by the Lords Proprietors to a woman, an Elizabeth Willis. Noteworthy, otherwise, for its most evident beauty, inside and out, it is fortunately built to last, with brick walls 29 inches thick, covered with oyster-shell stucco, and is paneled throughout with its original heart cypress. It also has a ghost, of a young poet who in 1786, outside the doorway, fought a duel over the famous actress, Perdita, and was brought inside the house to die. All very typically Charleston.

Within the white-paneled drawing room are rare pieces of Hepplewhite, Chippendale, Sheraton, an Adam mantel, an extraordinary old Tabriz animal carpet.

The color scheme for the dining room was taken from the Benjamin West portrait over the mantel; the chairs are Early American Regency made of mountain ash; the rug is an old floral needle point; and the camellias are from the garden.

Standing next to the old First Baptist Church, by Robert Mills, the house, now the residence of Mr. and Mrs. Henry Philip Staats, shows typical Charleston piazzas, the doorway leading into the lower piazza.

The Gibbes House

The face of the house is ornamented like an Adam mantel.

In the hallway, with its scenic paper, is a red Empire sofa.

. . . Facing out across the water from South Battery, it is amazing that this superb old mansion escaped injury from the bombardments of 1776 and 1861. It is one of Charleston's great residential monuments, the main floor standing a full story above the street, as though creating an excuse for the magnificent double staircase that decorates its Adamesque Georgian façade. Behind the house is a garden that glistens with white azaleas in the sunlight sprinkling down through the glossy leaves of great live oaks, and there are long, low servants' quarters and stables with shiny old tile roofs, so typical of Charleston.

The ballroom, which looks out across the Battery from the four right-hand windows of the top floor, is of course the showpiece of the house, but how to designate the showpiece of the ballroom is another matter: the spidery crystal chandelier? the immense Aubusson carpet? the plaster carving of the ceiling and cornice? . . . At any rate, other choice objects in the room are the early spinet and harp, rich brocades at the windows and on the furniture, and a gaming table said to have been used by Napoleon.

Wallpaper, decorations and even the English-detailed woodwork give the green drawing room (one of a pair on the main floor) a Chinese flavor.

Mulberry Plantation

Mulberry looks out over the Low Country from one of the locality's few hills.

THIS fascinating old house, of a most remarkable design, with four low corner towers, called flankers, of Jacobean baroque, and a generally sumptuous air, owes its opulence to the richness of the ancient rice fields down along the river. Its style and elegance can be credited to an early planter-politician, Thomas Broughton, who built it in 1714—some years before he really took title to the site; a lapse which causes local antiquarians still to raise their eyebrows.

But regardless of the manner in which Broughton acquired the property, the same authorities contend that as far as the house itself is concerned, the owner modeled it after the Broughton family seat in England. The old homestead must have been a house quite out of the ordinary, for Mulberry, as you can see, is not by any means the customary Colonial; in fact, it could be called unique. Principally, of course, because of the four little corner wings with their playful hoods above the lower hips, all topped with ornamental weather vanes. These wings, or flankers, have long been the cause of considerable controversy, one school of experts believing them to have some military significance, for the house did serve as a sort of fortress during various early wars with the Indians, and ancient cannon have been uncovered from what is now the lawn.

But other specialists point out that if these wings had been designed for defense, their large windows would have made them extremely vulnerable, even against arrows, and that slender slits in the brick would have offered more practical means of protection. At any rate, the flankers, for whatever they were meant, give the house great architectural charm, and provide breakfast room, study, office and pantry. The interior woodwork of the living and dining rooms is delicately Adam, and was probably installed by an owner in the early 1800's. The present owners have put the whole place in splendid condition—the lawns, walks, woods and waterside, as well as the house itself—and make Mulberry accessible in spring to the public as one of the loveliest relics of Low Country plantation life.

Beyond the dining room's Sheraton and Hepplewhite is one of the flanker rooms.

Mulberry's living-room furniture is mostly from the eighteenth century.

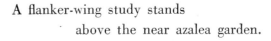

A flanker-wing study stands
　　　above the near azalea garden.

The carved staircase and main hallway, completely paneled in pine, are the climax of Carter's Grove's interiors, called the finest in America.
PRATT

Carter's Grove

This magnificent Colonial mansion, monumentally framed by enormous tulip poplars, faces out over the James from the topmost of its terraced lawns, six miles below Williamsburg. The downriver wing at the right was built in 1690; the upriver wing from five to ten years later; and the main central section between 1720 and 1730, when the English master builder, Richard Bayliss, was brought over to Virginia to design and carry out this most important part of the house, assisted by a fellow countryman, David Minitree.

From the land side Carter's Grove still has the plantation aspect—still functions as one. Looming larger and larger as you approach it through the fields, it rises beyond the lovely brick stables, growing more and more beautiful the closer you come.

Carter's Grove

It is typical of many Virginia mansions of the time that Carter's Grove was built of materials that for the most part were grown or manufactured right on the plantation. All the timbers and framing were cut from forests on the property, and all the famous paneling, of pine, walnut and poplar, was carved from lumber off the place. Even the bricks were baked on the site, of clay that was dug from the fields which lay between the house and the river. What transformed these local products into such a wonderful work of art was the taste and intelligence of Carter Burwell, who was proprietor of the plantation during the time that the principal construction was done. His taste produced, no doubt, the general idea, while his intelligence led him to bring a builder like Bayliss from London for the design and

In the paneled drawing room, a duel was fought. One killed, one wounded.

execution. Burwell could hardly have done better, as Carter's Grove today bears beautiful witness, both inside and out.

However, not all the handwork on the house was performed by such a skillful craftsman. One bit of carving—on the stair rail in the main hall—is a vivid reminder of an incident that took place in 1781, when a Colonel Tarleton, in command of the British Light Horse Cavalry, was occupying Carter's Grove—his troops occupied in raiding the countryside. It seems that one night, in his cups, the colonel mounted his horse, rode into the hall and up the stairs, slashing at the rail with his sword on the way. The cuts have been carefully preserved, of course, and are carefully pointed out to visitors. The colonel's workmanship may be British, but it can't compare with his countryman's carving, though for the sake of the legend it is almost as precious.

This simply furnished and paneled room is called the office, and as such it is used, serving also as an informal sitting room and study. Its more primitive appearance is due to the fact that it occupies the up-river wing, built twenty-five years or more before the main part of the house.

In the delightful setting of this drawing room, George Washington is said to have proposed to a Williamsburg girl named Mary Cary, and Thomas Jefferson to Rebecca Burwell. Because of the nature of the response that was given there in both cases, it is now known as the Refusal Room.

43

Sully's portrait of Peyton Randolph dominates the drawing room, with its original paneling and magnificent Aubusson.

BERKELEY

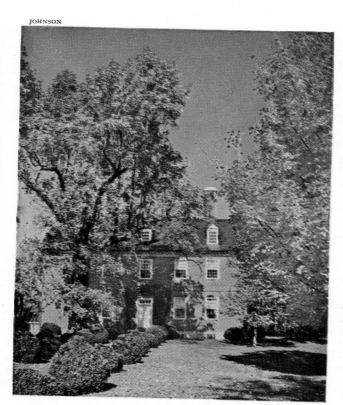

JOHNSON

The river front is a fine example of the early Georgian fashion.

Both Berkeley and Brandon have had their ups and downs during their long lives, but now, their careers have been resumed in the manner to which they were first accustomed. Berkeley has been more recently restored than its distinguished neighbor at some distance across the river, and was more of an undertaking, the outside of the older house at some point having been covered with plaster; and while it had never been shelled from British gunboats on the James, as Brandon was, still bearing the scars on its garden porch, it had been served rather ruthlessly at times, and its splendid condition today is a tribute to its present owners, who have had the courage to treat it colorfully to fine effect. Both houses, being private homes, are open to the public only during Virginia's annual garden pilgrimage.

Handsome archways connect the north drawing room with its counterpart on the opposite page, together called the "Great Room." Barrel chair is Sheraton.

Portrait of Benjamin Harrison, the "Signer," and once owner, looks out on the old English silver, Hepplewhite chairs, Waterford glass and Chinese porcelain.

Aubusson rug and Louis XV settee add a French touch to this section of the "Great Room." Other pieces are Sheraton and Chippendale.

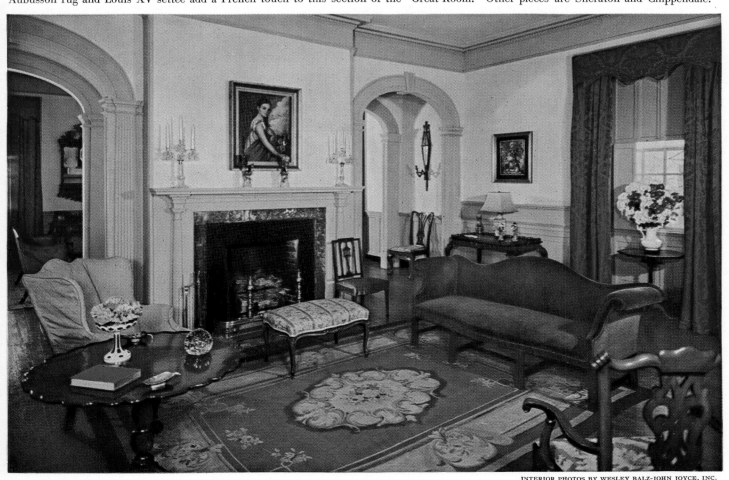

GUNSTON HALL

THE STORY OF FAMOUS OLD GUNSTON HALL, IN FAIRFAX COUNTY, VIRGINIA

JUST about the time George Washington was remodeling Mount Vernon for his marriage to Martha Custis, some friends of his, five miles down the Potomac, were moving into their brand-new house whose beauty today, while far less familiar to most of us than that of the first President's home, is still enough to take your breath away. Of course, when they walked into freshly finished Gunston Hall in the spring of 1758, the young George Masons were better prepared for the sight that met their eyes than anyone visiting the house for the first time now; they'd been watching it go up for a good three years. And it's practically certain that the general scheme of the house was pretty much George Mason's own; a knowledge of architecture then being part of any wealthy Virginian's possessions— along with plenty of money and slaves to put his notions into practice.

What Mason wanted in the way of a house, and what he got, as you can see, was a glorified Georgian cottage, much larger than it looks. Within the house, and without as well, he wanted the most wonderful woodwork to be seen in the Colonies, which in those talented times would take a lot of trying; but he succeeded in getting this too. The way he worked it was to send to London for a man named William Buckland, whose skill as a carver was unexcelled and whose knowledge of Classical ornament unsurpassed. Then Mason let Buckland loose with a simple Colonial plan to follow; gave him marvelous mellow white pine that would make your mouth water; hardwoods for framing which were seasoned to perfection; handmade oversize brick for the walls; limestone for the steps, foundations, corners—and hordes of help, falling all over themselves.

To this creation of that master craftsman and his perfectionist employer, time has now given a glow for which the Masons weren't able to wait. Life is too short. It must have seemed to them that the boxwood grew with tantalizing slowness; but

PHOTO BY PRATT

Across the parterred garden, laid out in the manner of the period by the present owner, the house rises above the age-old boxwood, a mansion of unusually modest appearance for a large manor house of the time.

PHOTO BY HAROLD FOWLER

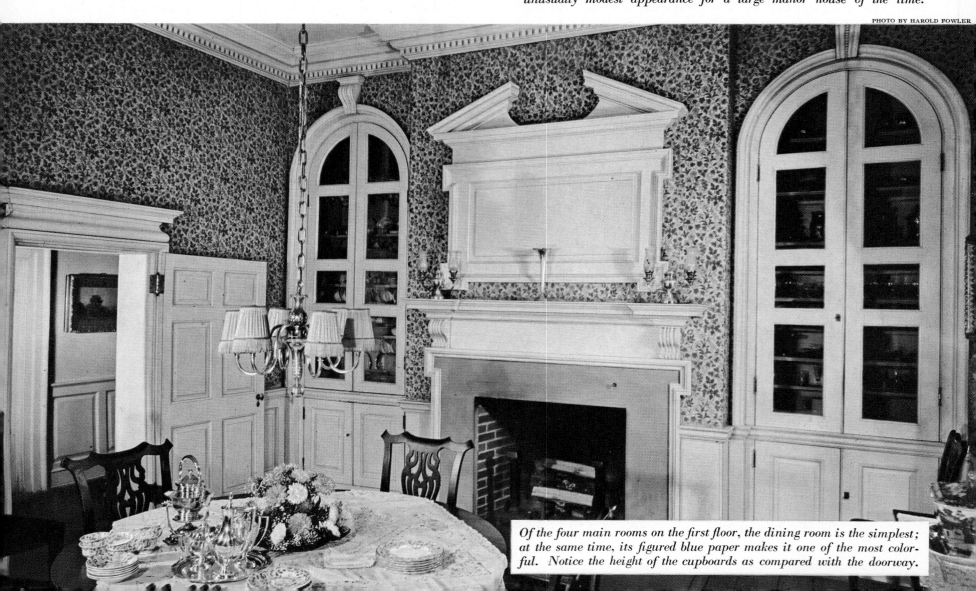

Of the four main rooms on the first floor, the dining room is the simplest; at the same time, its figured blue paper makes it one of the most colorful. Notice the height of the cupboards as compared with the doorway.

PHOTOS BY FOWLER

Furniture makes no effort to compete with the glorious wood carving of the Palladian room, unequaled in this country; woodwork set off by the pine-paneled walls, no less effectively than when the pine was originally covered with what was probably a figured damask—the tack holes still visible.

Above the mantel in the library is fixed a facsimile of the Virginia Declaration of Rights, the historic document written by George Mason, the original owner of Gunston Hall, who was a close friend and neighbor of George Washington.

The view through the doorway leading from the Chinese Chippendale room to the hallway not only indicates the unusual, and unusually beautiful, woodwork decoration of the room, but the spaciousness and dignity of the big entrance hall beyond.

Gunston
Hall
in
Virginia.

now, having had almost two centuries to attain its present monumental proportions, it has become the great feature of the grounds. And indoors, all this while, the passage of nearly two hundred years has given the woodwork an almost magical quality—or so it seems to eyes accustomed to the somber miracles of modern machinery. George Mason, whose body lies buried near the house, has given a glow himself to American history, as the author of the Virginia Declaration of Rights, the basis of our Constitution's Bill of Rights, and the major part of the Constitution of Virginia, and as a man whom Jefferson called the wisest of his generation. But when you walk into the drawing room of Gunston Hall, the brilliance you feel is Buckland. The handiwork of that inspired English carpenter is the light that lingers in your vision when you leave.

Listen briefly to the way I imagine he worked; it may add to the pleasure you get from his windows, doorways, cornices, mantels and porches. For here was a man with taste as well as talent in his fingers, plus a complete command of Classical ornament, which was then the dominating motif in all design. A piece of clear pine laid out upon his bench was like the keyboard of a piano under his hands. He could take his tools and carve out the equivalent of a Mozart sonata, except that the music he followed was the music of Palladio, Vitruvius and Chippendale, who composed in stone and wood. No workman remembered now carried with him a larger library of Renaissance engravings or a better collection of contemporary handbooks, and I think of them as resting on a shelf above his bench, and Buckland carefully wiping his hands before consulting their pages.

These books were the architects that sailed from England in the early days to guide the craftsmen here when it came to questions of style; and to these books can be traced all the characteristics of design which we now call Colonial or Georgian. In the hands of a man like Buckland, these books came to life; more wonderfully in certain ways at Gunston Hall than anywhere else I know, and most wonderfully there, in my opinion, in the Palladian room, or drawing room, and the demioctagonal porch on the garden side, with the Chinese Chippendale room competing for my preference. Purists among present-day traditional architects may be inclined to quarrel with some of Buckland's proportions—the window heights, the tallness of the cupboards; but to me these so-called disregardings of the rules are triumphs of individuality. They are what give Gunston Hall its extraordinary charm, vitality and distinction—qualities that should be seen face to face to be fully appreciated.

Anyone can go to Gunston Hall. It is the private residence now of Mr. Louis Hertle, to whom we are indebted for the privilege of photographing it for the pleasure of our readers. Mr. Hertle makes any interested and appreciative visitor feel welcome, and the walls of his library are lined with the autographed pictures of prominent people who have enjoyed his hospitality and friendship—from Franklin Roosevelt back to William Howard Taft. It was about the time of the latter that Mr. Hertle acquired Gunston Hall, restored it with great regard for its original aspect, and deeded it, as a monument to be preserved for posterity, to the Commonwealth of Virginia.

You cut in from Route 1, about fifteen miles below Alexandria, following a country road for several miles toward the east. You come to some simple gateposts, and a winding lane, and at the end of the lane you come to the house. If it is spring, and the dogwoods are in bloom, the house may seem to be standing in a soft, mysterious pool of light. But I have imagined this strange luminosity in midsummer, too, and in winter; so it may be merely the memory of Buckland. At any rate, you can't mistake the house. There is nothing quite like it anywhere else I know.

The porch that faces the gardens is a partial octagon in shape, and probably the only original porch of its kind in the country; an outstanding example of William Buckland's skill as an adapter and designer from classical models; for there is a theory that this design was derived from an engraving of a Roman coin that shows a similar feature in the Temple of Tyche in Eumeniea. From it you get a beautiful view of the gardens and look down the allée shown opposite.

From one of the bedrooms on the second floor you look down across the ancient box-bordered allée that separates the two parterred gardens, and over the intervening landscape to the Potomac and the shores of Maryland beyond. These gardens are beautiful all the year round, but they are at their best in the early spring, when the dogwoods and tulips are out.

By far the most outstanding feature of the grounds at Gunston Hall is the boxwood which, although it grows almost imperceptibly, has now attained impressive proportions in the course of nearly two centuries. It is especially effective in this allée from the garden house, overlooking the view toward the river, and the porch that appears close-up at the left on this page.

the choice examples of early American engines in the United States.

SOUTHERN MARYLAND

EXTERIOR PHOTOGRAPHS BY RICHARD PRATT.   INTERIOR PHOTOGRAPHS BY BALZ-SELWYN LTD.

Tulip Hill, with its widespread wings, looks out from its terraced hilltop in Anne Arundel County over almost a mile of farmland to the Chesapeake Bay.

IT is true that in Annapolis, where Southern Maryland begins, there are more well-set-up midshipmen to make the place attractive than grace any other American city. But it happens that Annapolis, compared with any other American city, also contains more handsome Georgian houses of great distinction; and it is really because of this fact, beyond everything else, that the town is beautiful. Then for further beauty, from the neighborhood of Annapolis, where the Severn opens into the Chesapeake, all the way down to the Potomac, the back roads of Southern Maryland lead you to more fine Georgian plantations than can be found in any other region of equal size in the country. You can take, as two superb examples of what you will find, Whitehall, on the opposite page, whose portico faces out across the bay just before you come to Annapolis; and Tulip Hill, above, which is the first great house you discover after you leave. From there on, among the rolling hills and along the tidewater rivers, farther and farther away from the Naval Academy, the only competition the houses get comes from the landscape itself, which plays right into the picture.

Walking through Annapolis streets, you meet one masterpiece after another. The prize, in my opinion, is the Hammond-Harwood house, shown two pages farther on, the work of the same William Buckland who was the master carpenter of Virginia's famous Gunston Hall, pictured on page 48. Directly across the street, the stately Chase house, shown at the right below, and near by the Brice and the Paca houses, the latter now part of Carvel Hall, the former now made into apartments for many families where once one family lived in grandeur. Even the street names, like the streets themselves, carry you back to Colonial times: King George, Prince George, and the Duke of Gloucester Street, where the Ridout house, at the left below, stands out as a major masterpiece along a streetful of minor ones—the minor ones on many streets serving as a connecting chorus throughout the town to the cast of principals.

The Ridout house, in Annapolis, famous for the purity of its proportions.

The Chase house is one of the noblest and tallest of the Annapolis mansions.

Whitehall, near Annapolis, in Anne Arundel County, was built in 1765, and its Corinthian portico is one of the oldest in the country.

Near the crossroads village of Friendship at the lower tip of Anne Arundel County, Holly Hill's appearance is somewhat misleading, for with its single-story eaves it looks like a small house, which it isn't. Otherwise, there is nothing misleading about its looks, it being one of the loveliest and most appealing of Southern Maryland's old country houses, from its brickwork and windows and cornice right up to its chimneys.

HOLLY HILL

Being one of the earliest of the Georgian houses in Southern Maryland, Holly Hill has had plenty of time to acquire a history. One legendary fragment is that it was used by a pirate named Hogarth who had dug an underground passage to Herring Bay, half a mile away, through which he carried plunder from his boats. The place the "passage" enters the cellar can still be seen but, as the tunnel now extends only ten feet from the house, skeptics are inclined to doubt the story's authenticity. No one could possibly doubt, however, the authenticity of Holly Hill's age and beauty. Records show that the house was begun in the seventeenth century and finished early in the eighteenth, and it is obvious that its beauty was built into it. The marbleizing which covers the entire wood-paneled end of the main bedroom at the left, and the painting on wood above the fireplace are indications of its unusually charming interior, which was beautifully restored to its pristine condition about ten years ago by its present owners. Some of the original window-panes bear the diamond-scratched signatures of the early occupants of Holly Hill. But as yet no signature of the pirate Hogarth has been found.

HAMMOND-HARWOOD HOUSE

This has been called the most perfect example of Georgian architecture in America, and the chances are that that is a fairly safe estimate of its standing in the great community of Colonial houses which line the Eastern seaboard from Maine to Charleston. The charm and dignity of its design, along with its incomparable carving, are all the creation of the master carpenter, William Buckland, who was introduced to Annapolis by George Mason after Buckland had made such a success of Mason's Gunston Hall in Virginia. Its restoration and maintenance have been made possible by the proceeds from the annual pilgrimage which every spring makes most of the great old houses in Maryland accessible to the public.

Every detail of the Hammond-Harwood house, in Annapolis, is a work of art. The principal rooms in the main section of the house are all celebrated for Buckland's beautiful woodwork, but the dining room, with its carved shutters, is the showpiece.

PHOTO BY PRATT

THE READ HOUSE IN NEW CASTLE, DELAWARE, *could probably be called the showpiece of the town. That it is as fresh and fine today as it was when it was finished in 1801 is largely due to the tender care that has been given it by its present owners, Mr. and Mrs. Philip D. Laird. As with most important American houses of the period, and before, it follows the then prevailing popular English Georgian style.*

PHOTOS BY KERTESZ

NEW CASTLE, DELAWARE

AT least by Colonial reckoning, New Castle, Delaware, was already a rather old town in 1791 when George Read II, fifteen years after his father signed the Declaration of Independence, started to build this stately mansion with bricks brought down the river from Philadelphia by barge. The house took ten years to build, but it was time well spent, for when Read's master craftsmen finally laid down their tools, they had put up something for posterity.

Here on these two pages, for part of that posterity, is the way the Read house looks today, after being lived in for a hundred and forty-five years. And on the next two pages are glimpses of the town around it, where in early summer the Green, with its buildings of mellow brick, lies under the lavender canopy of tall paulownias, and the shady little streets are tightly set with house after handsome house, all still brightly reflecting a scene of centuries gone by. It is something not to miss.

Yet every year half a million motorists, passing by less than a minute away, miss it by barely a hundred yards. This is largely because the *new* town of New Castle has drawn a cordon of ordinary streets and ordinary houses around all but the river side of the old town; creating a kind of camouflage, through whose effect of ordinariness you unsuspectingly press on toward Florida or Maine. But whether you are heading north or south on this particular highway that brushes the skirts of New Castle, you are bound to pause at this point anyway, for it is here that you ferry the Delaware. And coming across the river from the New Jersey side, if you look a little off to the left, you can't help catching sight of the pink and white and yellow rows that front the old town; and then farther back above the roofs a sparkling white spire and two lofty white cupolas to give the place completely away—to anyone with his wits about him.

At any rate, the street you see from the river is called The Strand, and the most striking house you see along The Strand from the ferry is the Read house shown here. It's a good street to start on, and the Read house is one of the first you meet, with its elegant Georgian façade facing out across the river. But when you look farther up The Strand, if you're anything like me, the lure of the town has caught you, and you make up your mind to give a quick preliminary glance at everything, then come right back for a longer look—and at everything else, all over again. You think if it's all been there this long, it will certainly stay for another few minutes—though you yet aren't sure it's absolutely real (and that's not just a way of talking).

By the time you've hurried up the fairly long unbroken block of The Strand, with your eyes popping out, you've made the full front width of the old town. One long block wide, and three shorter blocks back from the river, contain everything you want to see. You come to a broad open street and see first the town hall and courthouse,

Distinguished Colonial houses of old New Castle.

The great fanlight above the wide double doors, leading from the living room into the reception room, is a unique architectural feature of this famous house. The musical instrument is a harp guitar of the period, and in the oval frame is a picture of Robert E. Lee as a young Army officer. The mirror is Queen Anne.

In the upstairs hall you look out across the river through the Palladian window, the outside of which you see in the façade on the opposite page.

On the marvelous mantel, are Lowestoft urns. The Hepplewhite table by the window is flanked by a Hepplewhite and a Queen Anne chair.

The furnishings in the dining room were collected by the owners since they acquired the famous old house. Here the table is Duncan Phyfe, the chairs Chippendale and the sideboard Hepplewhite. The silver was made in London at the time the house was built. The scenic paper shows views of old New Castle.

New Castle, Delaware, is a town of rare distinction in this country because of its well-preserved antiquities and its atmosphere of centuries gone by.

each crowned with the cupolas you saw from the river; and behind them the Green, with its elms and paulownias; and down the Green the church and academy. And facing the Green, two streets of houses, whose dates you discover run from 1665 to 1830, give you a picture of the purity, simplicity and charm of the architecture that colored those hundred and sixty-five years. I don't know where else you would get so clear a picture so carefully preserved, so unself-conscious and unexploited, still living along, and living the life of today, as though it weren't a miracle that it was all still here.

The Read house is still there when you get back to The Strand—a house whose delicate, subtle yet vigorous details of trim on doorway, windows and cornice are rewarding things to look at closely if you are in the least affected by beautiful carving.

And if you are lucky enough, or foresighted enough, to have come to New Castle the third Saturday in May, you will have a chance to go inside the Read house, and any of the others you want. For that is the annual festival they call A Day in Old New Castle. In each house hostesses in costume welcome your call, and all doors are open, for an extremely modest over-all fee that goes to the local churches.

The feeling you get when you see inside the Read house is much the feeling you get when you wander round the town—a feeling of something having been very tenderly preserved, and of having been lived in with a very loving appreciation of its enduring quality. No preciousness here, or in the town as a whole. The Read house, as you can tell from the pictures, has been furnished as a home, and not as a museum. Likewise the town has always been treated as a town, and not as a tourist attraction, which of course accounts for the extraordinary attractiveness everywhere you look, inside and out.

You can look at all the old New Castle houses as closely as you like for all but a very few are flush against the pavements. You can reach out and feel the surface of the fine old brick and woodwork as you walk along the streets; get a close-up view of the beautiful variety of moldings and panelings on a multitude of windows and doorways, and examine the many designs of doorknockers, knobs and keyplates (which look as though they get a daily polishing). If hardware of this rare kind claims your attention, and you have a chance to look inside the Kensey Johns house on Orange Street, it is interesting to learn that the handles and keyplates on the main doors there have counterparts in only one other American house—Mount Vernon. In fact when a set disappeared from Mount Vernon, back in the Twenties, the owner of the Kensey Johns house gave up one of his to the Washington shrine—a delightful gesture from one fine old house to another.

Practically all the more distinguished New Castle houses are known by the names of their original owners: the Read, the Kensey Johns, the Van Dyke, the Nicholas Van Dyke, the Van Leuvenigh, the McWilliams. One, called the Amstel house, older than most, is now a museum; and one known as the Little Dutch House is the oldest of all—1665, or thereabouts—and is also a museum, which it well deserves to be. For this diminutive dwelling, which faces the Green, and is shown on the upper right-hand corner of the opposite page, was built right after the English had seized the whole district from the Dutch, the Dutch having taken it sometime before from the Swedes, who had earlier established the district that is now the state of Delaware, calling it New Sweden. The architectural flavor of New Castle is consequently English Georgian, though the work was done by colonial craftsmen.

But the houses aren't by any means the whole attraction of New Castle. The buildings that border both ends of the Green, and the Green itself, with its shadows and turf and trees, are just as much a trip into the past as the homes along the shady streets. My favorite is the foursquare town hall and market, which you see when you first come round the corner from The Strand. Its street level is pierced through the center by a vaulted passage that once led to a market in the rear. From there it rises with fine Georgian dignity and great simplicity of style to the handsome cupola that caps the roof. Under another handsome cupola, the courthouse, right next to the town hall, is the most impressive structure in the town; its main central section in scale with its importance, its flanking wings of more domestic proportions; giving it a close relationship with the rest of its surroundings. Then at the other end of the Green, the church and the school stand in a pool of peace and quiet unusual even for New Castle—stand just as beautifully now, and as usefully, too, as they have stood for almost two hundred years.

That so much of New Castle remains is largely due to the fact that ever since the time of the town's greatest importance as a thriving center of government and commerce, which was just about when the Read house was built, the industrial activities of progress have more or less passed it by, like the motorists pressing on toward Florida and Maine. Having led a life of comparative calm, it is consequently well preserved. But its preservation is also due to the people who live there and love it, and to local organizations which help support and direct an active public interest in the whole historical aspect of the community.

It is still not too late for many other Colonial communities, once rich in landmarks of everlasting value, to learn from New Castle

School and church down the Green.

The rear of the public buildings beyond the paulownias.

The courthouse still functions after two centuries.

The masterful town hall and old market.

The Little Dutch House, oldest in New Castle, is now a historical museum.

With its pedimented doorway and twenty-four-paned windows, the Kensey Johns house, which faces the Green from Orange Street, is one of the most purely proportioned in the town.

A row of old houses on The Strand; and below, a typical view of New Castle back yards, looking from The Strand toward the town hall and courthouse.

HOUSES IN THE PARK

EXTERIOR PHOTOGRAPHS BY RICHARD PRATT, INTERIOR PHOTOGRAPHS BY WESLEY BALZ—JOHN JOYCE, INC.

Few Colonial façades were as richly designed as Mount Pleasant, with its brickwork quoins, its Palladian window above its bold Tuscan doorway.

MOUNT PLEASANT

IT is little wonder that back in Colonial days, and on after the Revolution, the hills shouldering out above both banks of the winding Schuylkill were favored spots for wealthy Philadelphians on which to build their country seats and summer homes. The sites were beautiful and cool, and although the going was bad between there and town, with a barouche and pair you could drive out from Independence Hall in less than an hour. Now, of course, by car or bus it is a matter of minutes, and the trip is unforgettable, for the region has been devotedly preserved as perhaps the largest and finest city park in the country, and the old mansions that adorn its hills are protected by the park forever; nine or ten of the best being open for you

to see, most handsomely maintained—perfectly in the manner to which they were accustomed in those elegant early times.

Of all the houses in the Park, Mount Pleasant is the most imposing, for John Macpherson, who built it in 1761, was lavish with the money he made from privateering, and expense was no object. Then, too, Philadelphia artisans were men of extraordinary taste and talent, and the house inside and out is a monument to their skill: boldly conceived and brilliantly executed. In 1779 it passed from Macpherson to Maj. Gen. Benedict Arnold, at that time the American commander at Philadelphia, who bought it for his bride, the famous beauty, Peggy Shippen; but he never had a chance to occupy it.

Philadelphia's Fairmount Park is the fortunate possessor of a half score of famous old houses, furnished and decorated to period perfection for everyone to see. Here on these eight pages are four of the finest.

The upper hall, a tour de force of Ionic detailing.

The dining-room chairs are Philadelphia Chippendale.

The great chamber above the dining room is the most richly ornamented room in the house. Queen Anne tables and side chairs; Chippendale wing chair.

The pent eaves show where the second story was added in 1756.

The maple drawing room contains every possible period accessory.

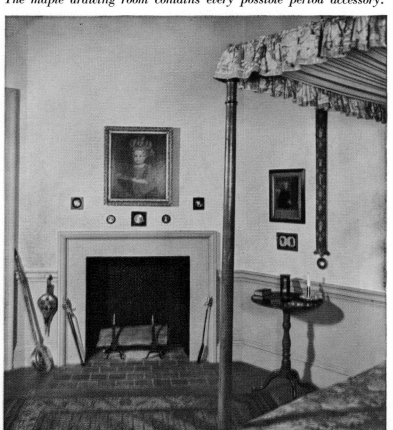

WOODFORD

A BEAUTIFUL example of Colonial mansion, Woodford is also a splendid one of the way these rare heritages of this country's past can be preserved for all Americans, now and forever. Already permanently owned by the city of Philadelphia and protected by its location within Fairmount Park, it had the further good fortune to be entrusted about twenty years ago to the estate of Miss Naomi Wood, a native Philadelphian who had left an extraordinary collection of Colonial furniture and furnishings to be placed in an appropriate house. Woodford was the house selected, and here not only have her practically priceless pieces been beautifully installed, but through her additional bequests the house has been completely equipped in every detail, as if for Colonial occupancy, with the result that Benjamin Franklin might just have been having tea in the drawing room opposite, as in fact he often did have it in days gone by. Few early-American houses have been so handsomely endowed, and so impeccably arranged, to give the feeling that the Colonial occupants had just gone out for a walk. Everything beautifully belongs. The drawing room, for instance, is furnished largely in walnut, cut from the groves that lined the near-by Schuylkill and wrought by the fabulous craftsmen of eighteenth-century Philadelphia: the 1760 Queen Anne armchair, the American Chippendale wing chair with a walnut Chippendale piecrust candlestand beside it; and of course with all the original carving of the room itself intact. The upstairs drawing room, seen in the middle at the left, is done entirely in maple, of Philadelphia furniture of the period, mostly in the Queen Anne, Sheraton and Jacobean styles, which local craftsmen created as skillfully as their colleagues in London.

The drawing room where Benjamin Franklin often came to tea.

The bedroom, with a perfectly treated fireplace wall and mahogany bed.

PHOTO BY PRATT

A HOUSE WHERE WASHINGTON REALLY SLEPT

One of the prize exhibits in the Litchfield collection of houses, in terms of both legend and beauty, is the one known for more than a century as Sheldon's Tavern. It was at first somewhat simpler in outward appearance when erected by Elisha Sheldon in 1760, and remained so when Sheldon's son turned it into a tavern twenty years later. Then about 1800 it was worked upon by an architecturally talented pioneer Connecticut builder named William Spratt, who gave it the impressively columned entrance with the graceful Palladian window and pediment above, together with the cornices under the eaves and over the first-story windows, adding, as you can see, considerable style of a most agreeable kind. It was in the upstairs bedroom to the right of the Palladian window, and before that feature was put on, that Washington, on his way through New England, spent at least one night and maybe more; the four-poster in which he slept still is in use.

On either side of the entrance hallway of the house still spoken of as Sheldon's Tavern are two companion drawing rooms, the one here at the right being also the one at the right as you come in. The scale of the furniture is beautifully in keeping with the size of the room, whose delicately handled woodwork complements the paper as effectively as the mellow old floor boards set off the colorful bold patterns of the hooked rugs. The pieces are all Early American of the period of the house, the spinet under the mirror at the right having been made just about the time this house was built.

PHOTOS BY FOWLER

The drawing room below, at the left as you enter the house opposite, is largely paneled in painted pine, a perfect foil for the colorful glitter of a gold-framed embroidery piece and an eighteenth-century American mirror. The secretary is a fine example of sophisticated Colonial craftsmanship.

THE TAPPING REEVE HOUSE IN LITCHFIELD

PRATT

Later Colonial in Connecticut.

One of the most finely proportioned and gracefully treated houses in Litchfield is the one Judge Reeve built for himself in 1773, and to which he brought his bride, the sister of Aaron Burr. It was here, also, that he entertained the great Frenchman, Lafayette; and it was in the garden next to the house that he built his famous little law school, the first in the country, which is pictured on page 77. In its beautifully furnished rooms you will get a good idea of what others of the town's interiors are like.

The large, low-ceilinged living room of the Tapping Reeve house, its walls appropriately papered, provides a perfect setting for furnishings contemporary with the house, all part of the Litchfield tradition. The Governor Winthrop desk is one which Judge Reeve used. Note above the noteworthy mantel the Early American clock, the luster vases, the crystal lamps. Flanking the fireplace are a four and a five-slatted ladder-back chair, and through the doorway you can see the fabulous sideboard of the dining room.

FOWLER

PHOTOS BY FOWLER

In the southwest bedroom of the Reeve house the dominating piece is, of course, the graceful tester bed with its early Connecticut quilt. But very fine indeed are the delicate Windsor chairs, while the Colonial hatbox covered with squirrel paper is an appropriately decorative note. The painted-pine paneling naturally sets the furniture off to the best advantage, as well as the gold-framed embroidery which hangs above the old brick fireplace.

The honeylike pine paneling of the Tapping Reeve study, with its fluted pilasters and its rosetted capitals, gives extraordinary style and color to one of the mellowest and most appealing rooms in the famous old house. The tall-backed Windsor chairs, one of them curve-backed, one square, are once-in-a-lifetime pieces, and are wonderfully constructed for comfort, strength and character, like the Litchfield houses for which they were made.

PORTSMOUTH
New Hampshire

The house above was twenty-one years old in 1779, when John Paul Jones, for whom it is now named, boarded in it while his ship, America, was being fitted out in Portsmouth Harbor. Below, on Middle Street, just off Haymarket Square, from left to right, are the Thompson house, 1808; the brick Larkin house, 1815; the wood Larkin house, 1800; and the Langley Boardman house, 1800—quite a cluster.

THERE are parts of Portsmouth which can cast a spell so powerful that only the great old houses catch the eye, as fresh and bright as ever, seeming to make all signs of contemporary traffic disappear like magic from the sight of the captivated beholder. It would be no more than fair to say, however, that for these pictures, taken from the streets, the absence of traffic was made possible through the kind cooperation of Portsmouth people operating, it would appear, under the same spell with which the various lovely scenes in their city envelop the visitor. As plentiful as these distinguished and time-dispelling vistas are today in Portsmouth, on which in this book we can only make a start, there would have been many more but for a fire that swept the town in 1813. On the other hand, there would have been many fewer if Portsmouth, somewhat later, like most other early American cities, had been swept by the wave of nineteenth-century industrial prosperity under which so much of the charm and splendor of the past elsewhere all but vanished. For while Portsmouth today hums with activity, its period of fullest bloom was the romantic era of the sailing ships; famous fleets of which from all over the world she not only harbored but built superbly in the yards that lined her Piscataqua River, leading out to the Atlantic a few miles away. Now, of course, her tall, proud sails are gone, but there are mansions of the early mariners and merchants which still stand, as you can see, high and handsome, on her shady streets.

83

INTERIOR PHOTOGRAPHS BY HAROLD FOWLER. EXTERIOR PHOTOGRAPHS BY JAMES R. JOHNSON.

The arched niche in the elaborately carved and papered dining room holds a Hepplewhite sideboard; the chairs are Chippendale, the table an unusually fine Duncan Phyfe. The silver and the mirror are early American; the fruit dish and cake plate on the table are Staffordshire; and the rug is Chinese.

The principal bedroom is papered in a Colonial Chinese pattern; the four-poster is Chippendale; the magnificent cherry chest-on-chest is early American; the chairs are Hitchcocks; and the English tilt-top table stands on an early American hooked rug of about 1825. Beyond is the beautiful upstairs hall with its broad view of the river.

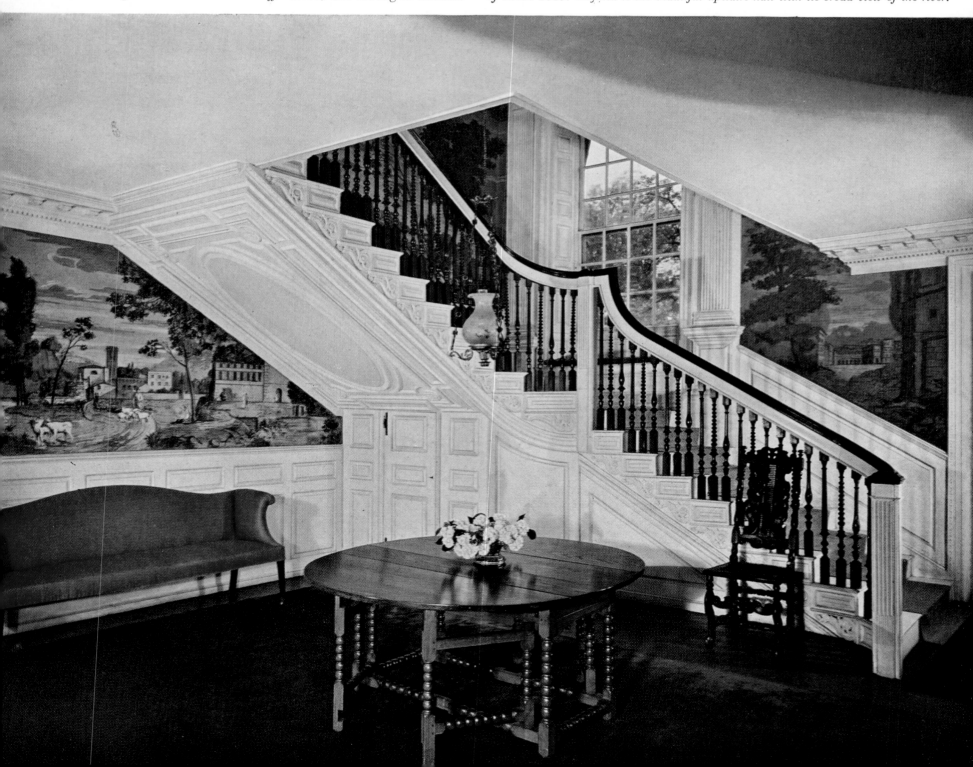

THE MOFFATT-LADD HOUSE

From the ship room on the second floor of his stately mansion, Captain Moffatt could look down upon his wharves below the bluff in front of the house and watch his ships sailing out the Piscataqua, bound for the four corners of the globe. The low building to the right is the office where his shipping affairs were conducted, affairs of much more magnitude than the size of the office would indicate, to have enabled him to build and maintain his home in such splendid style. Still owned by his descendants, the house has been placed in charge of the New Hampshire Society of the Colonial Dames, who have furnished it in the fashion to which it was accustomed.

Probably the most spacious and impressive hallway in New England, with one of the most beautiful staircases, the walls are covered with rare old Bay of Naples paper. The English gate-leg table antedates the house, the chair is Jacobean, the sofa Hepplewhite.

THE YOUNG REPUBLIC

Thomas Jefferson (1743–1826)

The Classical Look

in America

IN DECLARING their architectural independence from England, American houses after the Revolution were really announcing a new allegiance, this time to the Classic models of Greece and Rome. Our Georgian Colonial was derived directly from English sources, though its manners here became distinctly American. And although Thomas Jefferson, at the forefront in the change in taste, made quite a point of bypassing any field of English influence in the matter of design, going straight to Palladio for inspiration and instruction, the fact remains that England was inadvertently in various ways responsible for the wave of Classicism which covered the young republic; particularly in the form of published material—engravings of Classical examples from Italy and Greece, builders' handbooks adapting the Classic styles to domestic design, and literary works which sparked the Classic urge. When Nicholas Biddle, for example, decided to put up Andalusia in the image, more or less, of the Temple of Poseidon, it was an English engraving of this magnificent ruin at Paestum which was followed, rather than the ruin itself. More and more Americans of taste and influence were by the nineteenth century spending time in France, where the Empire had wrapped itself in a Classic mantle, and were traveling in Italy and Greece—Jefferson foremost among them—to observe the Classic models face to face. But English was our language;

we couldn't shake that loose; it still provided our most practical connection with the past. For it was from English books, more than from English models, that we drew our inspiration.

What we did with the Classic Revival here was something else again; something more American than anything before; leaving all the rest of the world behind in the exuberance and abundance with which we took to the temple form. The nation was growing up in many ways, but we were inclined to treat the Greek Revival like a toy, giving a Classic naïveté to hundreds of towns that sprang up as our population spread westward past the Alleghenies. On the other hand, many of the houses we built, particularly in the earlier part of the period, were outstandingly adult in their design, and mark many high points in American craftsmanship, betokening in their furnishing and decoration an awareness of the world at large. This awareness is keenly felt in what were then provincial places, like Natchez and New Orleans, where an aristocracy of wealth in many cases kept in closer touch with the Continent than with our own Eastern cities, as the houses show.

As far as architecture was concerned, the period had a personality of its own. It has been customary at times to call it all Colonial, but a look at the houses which follow should make it clear that the yearnings expressed could occur only in a nation that was beginning to feel its greatness.

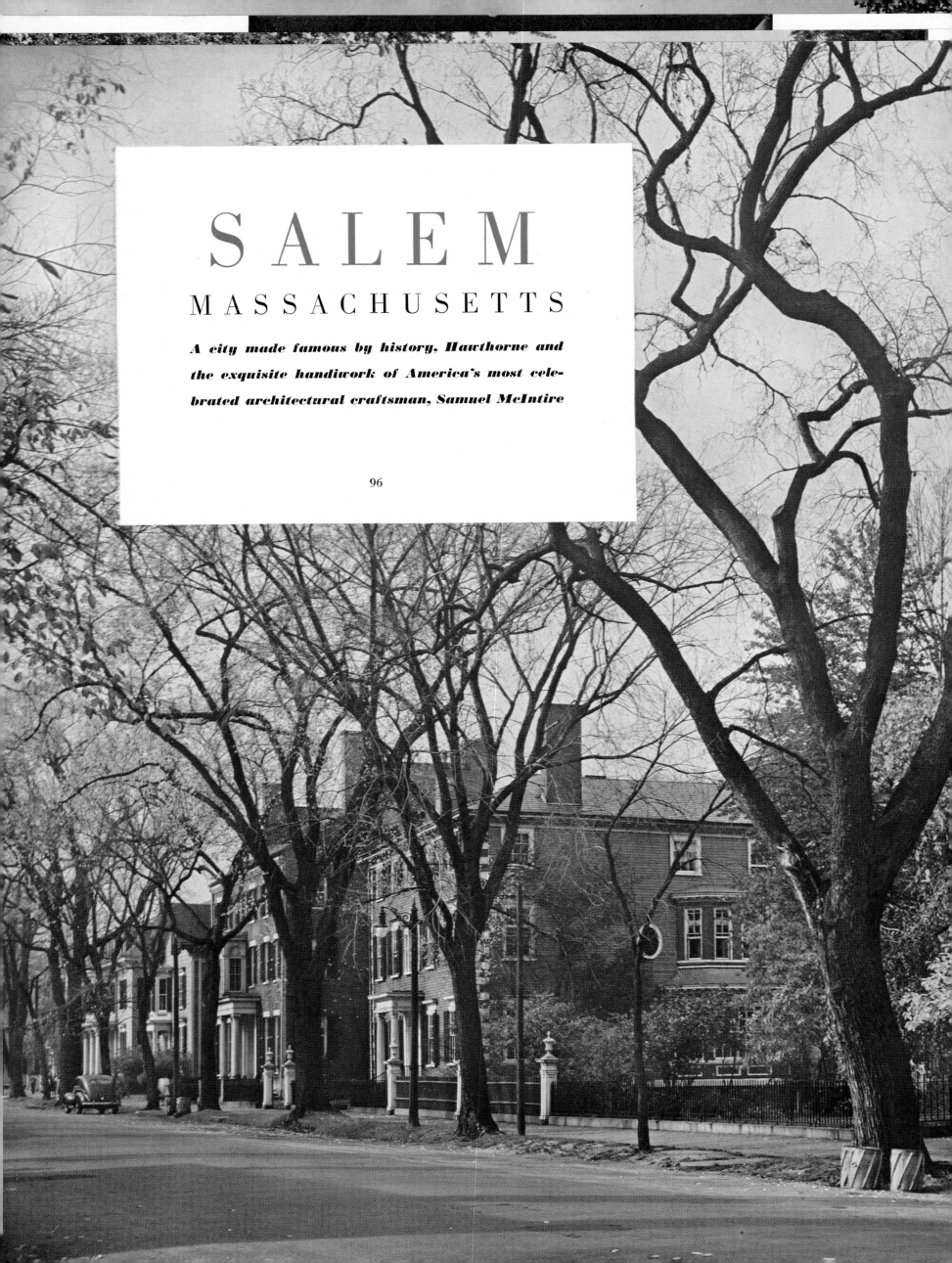

SALEM
MASSACHUSETTS

A city made famous by history, Hawthorne and the exquisite handiwork of America's most celebrated architectural craftsman, Samuel McIntire

96

SALEM'S memories begin with the Puritans, who settled there just six years after the landing at Plymouth Rock. And as far as posterity is concerned at present, those memories come to a climax with The Scarlet Letter, which was written on Mall Street there in the late 1840's by a sad, shy Salem man who had recently lost his job as surveyor of the port in the local customs office. In between, as you will recall, there was witchcraft. And there were the fabulous years of sailing ships, when riches from every region of the earth were heaped on Salem wharves, and Salem homes reflected the wealth of Salem merchants. These homes reflected, too, the talents of a Salem young man, a woodcarver by trade, with an extraordinary aptitude for architecture, whose taste and skill account for most of the major beauty which meets the eye in Salem today. For while in his comparatively short lifetime Samuel McIntire couldn't possibly have executed all the fine homes which Salem once possessed, it can be said that for all the best work in the great Salem tradition he was certainly the inspiration. The two great men of Salem never met; their lives overlapped too little. McIntire began the Pingree house, which appears on pages 100 and 101, in 1804, the year Hawthorne was born; and seven years later McIntire died at fifty-four. All his life was lived, and all his work was done, within a few miles of his native city; and it is a credit to Salem that there, in the midst of so very much now which scarcely measures up to McIntire, some of the master's finest achievements are still tenderly preserved. And for all that remain, the most outstanding, in my opinion, are the two which follow.

PHOTOGRAPHS BY PRATT

One long block of Chestnut Street is lined on both sides by Salem's largest remaining cluster of homes for which McIntire was directly or indirectly responsible.

Because of these capacious, foursquare houses, beautifully designed in the fashion of the Federal period, Chestnut Street has been called the architecturally finest residential street in America.

Woodstock architecture from the start, while the quality of its design, which remained remarkably high until about a hundred years ago, and has been a good influence ever since, can be credited to the carpenter craftsmen who worked their way inland from places like Portsmouth and Boston, where they had learned their trade among a multitude of earlier American masterpieces.

Now, as you amble under the elms of the famous Green, and turn the corner at the end down Elm Street, the past comes pleasantly to life, and you feel it is in safe hands here forever.

THE
WARREN-KIDDER
HOUSE

This house, around the corner from the Green, on Elm Street, was built in 1807 by Simon Warren, descendants of whom have occupied it ever since, through four generations, a record characteristic of Woodstock. It is of frame, with typical New England narrow clapboards, and a porch in the Federal style so popular when the house was put up. Certain fanciful touches, like the scroll of the central dormer and the variturned balusters of the staircase, give the impression that the carpenter craftsmen who worked on these features back in 1807 must have enjoyed their job. And the house has remained to give enjoyment to everyone who passes it and has a chance to look inside; for within, quite apart from the staircase that marches up in three-tone chords, every room contains distinguished pieces of fine old furniture, much of it having been handed down from one generation of the family to the next through the long history of the house.

Above the Federal porch, a Palladian window and a scroll-topped dormer.

ANDALUSIA

THE GREEK REVIVAL AT ITS BEST

BACK in the early part of the last century, Greece was fighting for her life against the Turks; and so frenzied were the feelings here in her behalf that there was talk of organizing private armies to help her, and towns from Maine to Florida were taking Attic names like Alpha, Athens, Euclid, Delta, Sparta, Troy and Ypsilanti. And houses all the way to the Mississippi began to look more or less like temples of the gods, creating a fashion that carried right up to the fifties, with results that ran from almost sublime to nearly ridiculous—a fashion now known as the Greek Revival. You must have seen at least some of its houses, with their serious Classic porticos, their columns and pilasters; and if you are at all familiar with the 1830 towns of Western New York, Northern Ohio and Southern Michigan, you

must have seen quite a few. But unless you have been fortunate enough to have seen Andalusia, you have missed the most important dwelling of the period. So here it is.

The broad lawns of Andalusia sweep down to the Delaware not far up the river from Philadelphia, with hardly anything to meet the eye that wouldn't have met it in the 1830's. And looking up from the river bank, you see what appears to be the Temple of Poseidon, translated into wood from the famous remains left by the Greeks at Paestum, now pillowed against Pennsylvania trees, and giving Classic grandeur to a fine old Pennsylvania mansion whose rooms live up in every way to the promise of that splendid portico. But before we look inside, let me tell you how it happened.

EXTERIOR PHOTOGRAPHS BY RICHARD PRATT   INTERIOR PHOTOGRAPHS BY BALZ-SELWYN LTD.

Looking up at a corner of the great Doric portico at Andalusia, its painted woodwork feels absolutely right as the face for this large and livable mansion.

One of the two yellow drawing rooms at Andalusia, glowing with gilt and decorated with Greek details of the period on overmantel and the surrounding cornice.

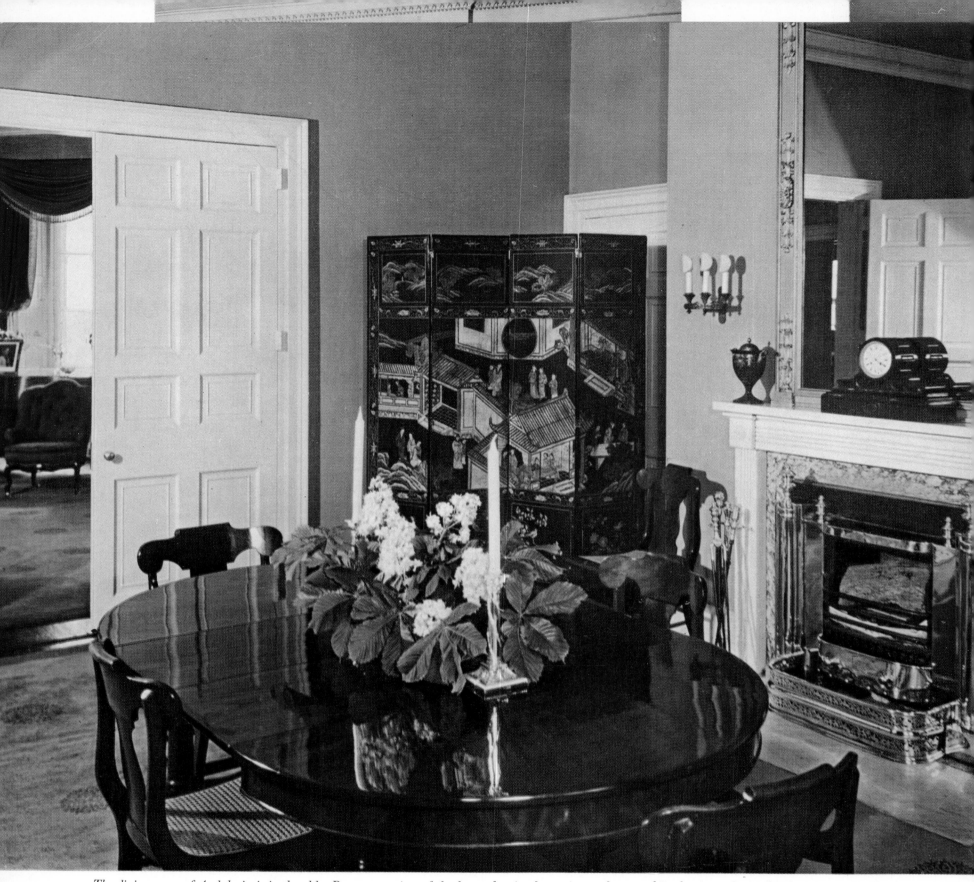

The dining room of Andalusia is in the older Regency section of the house, but its decoration and most of its furniture discreetly place it in the subsequent period of the famous Greek Revival addition. On the marvelously polished mahogany Empire table is an arrangement of horse-chestnut blossoms and branches.

had extraordinary warmth, and in spite of its immense proportions, had really livable scale.

There were to be even more ambitious achievements than Andalusia in the way of Classic emulation, of which Berry Hill, in Virginia, is an outstanding example, it being completely surrounded by columns, like the Parthenon.

But strangely enough, the temple effect in almost every house that followed Andalusia took on a residential quality; quite digni-fied, of course, in many cases, but amazingly homelike, considering the fact that the original temples were never designed for living. Leave it to the ingenuity of American carpenters and architects of the time to have made the transformation, though they could hardly have helped it if they were going to reduce the proportions to fit plain people, use wood instead

of stone, and provide regular doors and windows, along with chimneys, downspouts and all the other domestic devices. And as you have probably noticed, most of our Greek Revival houses are far less pure in style than Andalusia, which bears a remarkable resemblance to the original temple that Biddle chose to adapt. The liberties which carpenters took with the Greek details in a great majority of cases often produced a noteworthy naïveté and romantic charm—produced, in fact, a style that was eminently American, just as English Georgian had earlier, in this country, be-come Colonial.

The liberties taken grew greater as the Greek Revival went on, with more and more results that now seem rather quaint and amusing; until finally, in the fifties, people's preoccupation with Classic forms gave way entirely to the craze for Gothic. But that is quite another story.

The great garden of Andalusia, with its flowing trees, lies between two high walls, draped with wistaria.

The bookcases, painted with Classic decoration of the period, and the elegant old fruit-wood sofa, are features of the Biddle library at Andalusia.

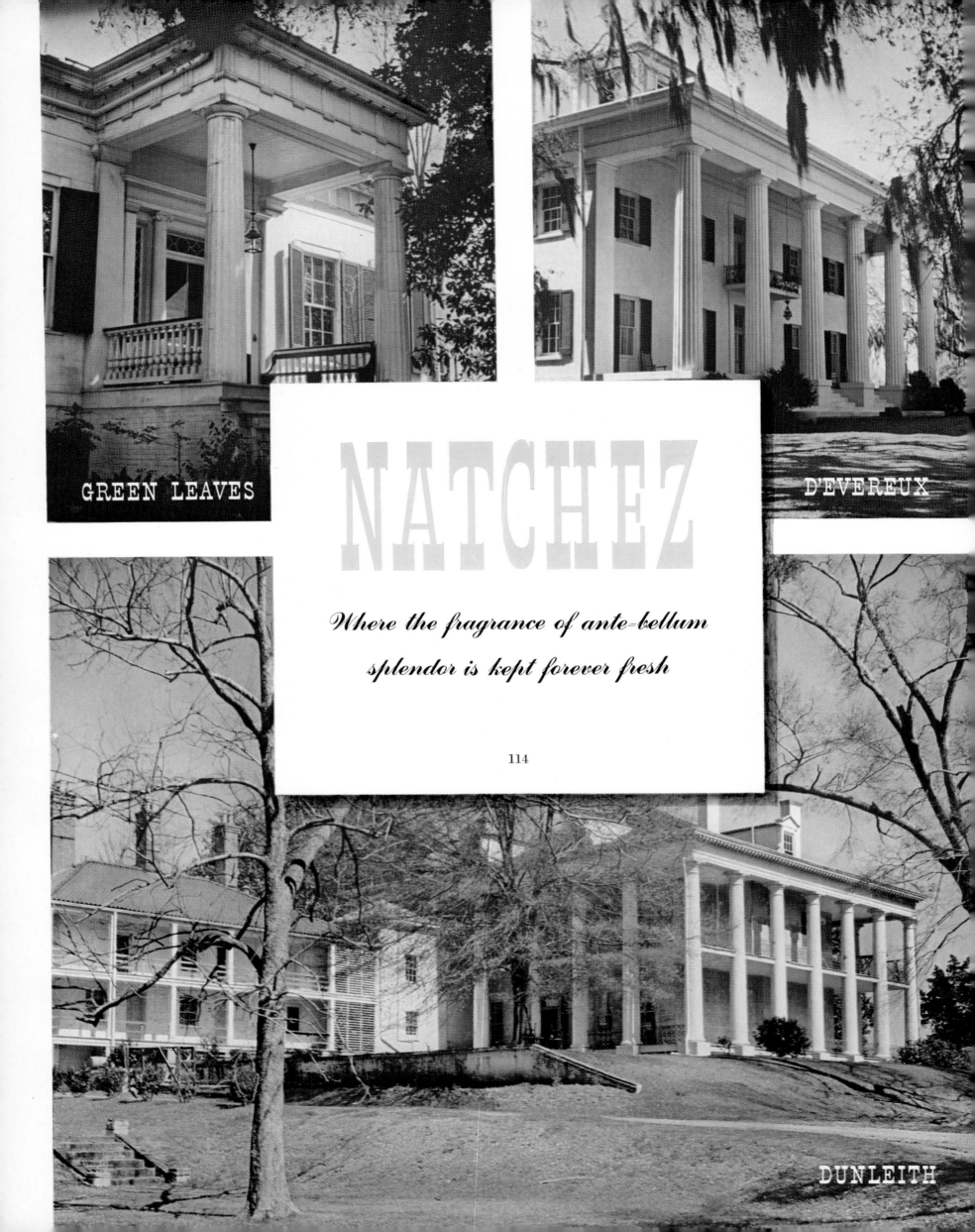

GREEN LEAVES

D'EVEREUX

NATCHEZ

Where the fragrance of ante-bellum splendor is kept forever fresh

114

DUNLEITH

EXTERIOR PHOTOGRAPHS BY RICHARD PRATT; INTERIOR PHOTOGRAPHS BY HAROLD FOWLER

The small library at Gloucester has an eighteenth-century mantel from France, Meissen garnitures from Germany, a secretary from England and paintings from Italy—typical of the importations of the time.

GLOUCESTER

The names of Natchez homes are part of their romantic flavor. Green Leaves, D'Evereux and Dunleith; Gloucester, Monteigne, Monmouth and Arlington; Longwood, Lansdowne, Linden, Rosalie, Hope Farm, Stanton Hall and Elgin; Richmond, Airlie, Mistletoe, and on and on: names and houses ornamenting the old town that stands high above the brown Mississippi and decorating the lush surrounding countryside. Gloucester is a good beginning, for it was the home of the first territorial governor, a rigid New Englander, named Winthrop Sargent, who came to this already colorful community about 1800, tried his Yankee best to resist its blandishments, and finally gave in to its luxurious delights. He now lies buried beneath a great magnolia on the lawn of his house whose Georgian manner he might have brought with him from Massachusetts—a style that the climate of Natchez embellished after its own exuberant fashion.

The upholstered pieces in the yellow drawing room at Gloucester show the effect of the Victorian fashion which found the Natchez homes such willing and wonderful settings for its romantic elegance.

MONTEIGNE

Younger than most of the Natchez homes, Monteigne was scarcely ten years old when Union soldiers were stabling their horses in its drawing rooms. But it survived this Civil War vandalism, and its condition today, as you can see, is practically perfect, its classic portico rising as proudly as ever before its beautifully proportioned pink façade. Set against a background of enormous live oaks, Monteigne is surrounded by great gardens of roses, camellias and azaleas, the soft night air heavy with their sweet smells and the daytime brilliant with their blossoms. In point of time, Monteigne marks the close of the golden age of Natchez, much as Hope Farm and Gloucester marked its beginning. From the end of the eighteenth century to the start of the Civil War, the Natchez district was peopled with families of fabulous wealth who loved to live elegantly. The ships which carried their cotton to the Eastern seaboard, to England and the Continent, carried them, too, and brought them back with the finest of furnishings for their homes and with the most cosmopolitan ideas for an idyllic life in this faraway community.

The guest bedroom at Monteigne is dominated by its chinoiserie chintz; its great tester bed and rosewood chairs in the best imported Victorian taste of the times.

Generations of hand polishing have produced a rich patina on the fine eighteenth-century furniture of the Monteigne dining room, where the light glitters on lavishly scaled repoussé silver and a delicate Venetian chandelier. Especially fine is the pair of Sèvres vases on the mantel.

Monteigne's entrance hall, with its marble floor, its harplike balustrade and its hand-blocked French scenic wallpaper, is one of the most stunning eye-catchers in the whole stunning Natchez neighborhood.

GREEN LEAVES

The twin parlors of Green Leaves, of which the room above is one, are identical except for details in their priceless accessories. The Beltzhoover family makes everyday use of both rooms, amid the Meissen and Sevres, the Watteau fans, the ivory miniatures, rare prints and manuscripts, and autographed albums of Confederate generals and other memorabilia of the War Between the States. And in the game room at the left it is as though time had stood completely still for a hundred years or more.

ARLINGTON

More than a century ago the library at Arlington *(left above)* was filled with eight thousand rare volumes, purchased in London, meticulously cared for ever since on the shelves that surround the room, whose tremendous scale is given away by the armchair in the corner. In the room at right, the present owner of Arlington keeps her famous collection of glass, the shelves having been effectively set against the windows of the gallery to bring out the beauty of old Bristol, Bohemian, Waterford and English crystal.

THE ELMS The back parlor at The Elms still has its original Victorian furniture intact, still upholstered in the now-seldom-seen original Windsor patterns. Also seldom seen nowadays are such items as the lily sconces above the mantel and the graceful rosewood escritoire. The bell pull beside the window rings its specially toned bell in the pantry, where each room has its own bell.

LINDEN Most Natchez homes had punkahs, or breeze fans, in their dining rooms, swung gently back and forth with strings by colored boys during the midday dinner, which is still the principal meal in Natchez homes.

LANSDOWNE The drawing room at Lansdowne represents the nineteenth century at its most fabulous, with a double set of rosewood furniture from France still covered in its original brocade. Imported at the same time as the furniture were the hand-painted wallpaper, the carpet, cornices and brocatels, making in all one of the most remarkable rooms of its period in the country.

VIEUX CARRÉ . . . *The streets in the old quarter have names like Iberville, Toulouse, Bienville, Bourbon, Dumaine and Chartres; and as you walk along under the lacy galleries you hear snatches of Creole French, and look through dark passageways into patios filled with sunlight and palms. Off the end of the street ahead, the Cathedral of St. Louis flanks a luxuriant square; and a few steps farther on oysters Rockefeller and the trout Marguery are as out-of-this-world as the Quarter itself.*

BLANC HOUSE . . . *Northwest of the Quarter, along Bayou St. John, are some of the early West Indian plantation houses, of which this is by far the most striking.*

BUCK HOUSE . . . *The symmetry and generous proportions of Garden District houses make an effective foil for their costumes of color and shadow.*

NEW ORLEANS

YOU can see what Thackeray and Mark Twain meant when they called this a Paris in America—which it isn't exactly; but the flavor of the famous old Creole Quarter is decidedly French provincial; and for a flavor of another sort you encounter in farther parts of the city occasional countrylike plantation houses that are marvelous in the moonlight; while in what they call the Garden District, where the air is scented with sweet olive blossoms, and the houses give off an aroma of antebellum elegance in settings of almost tropical lushness, you find still another flavor, that could be called crinoline. Altogether, it makes a unique and romantic potpourri, French, Spanish, English, named New Orleans. With the accent on the *Or*.

123

ROBINSON HOUSE . . . *In the Garden District, as well as the Quarter, many houses decorate themselves with delicate ironwork like lacy overlays for a valentine.*

PIRATE'S ALLEY . . . *Like a little street in the south of France. Notice that French Quarter façades may be repaired, but never modernized.*

In the old days the main central part of the house was the domain of the parents and daughters; the wings were the garçonnière, or quarters for the sons of the family and for the steady stream of guests who came by horse and carriage from the city and from plantations surrounding the countryside.

ORMOND PLANTATION

A FEW miles up the Mississippi River from New Orleans in a wide sweeping bend of the river, this plantation house, as you approach it from the road below the levee, appears very much as it must have looked when it went up, although the brick wings were added later. Built by the Butler family in the 1780's, its wide galleries clearly show a Spanish influence; its columns are typical of Louisiana.

THE LOWER HALL *leads from the entrance through a broad archway into a kind of casual sitting room that in turn leads out upon a garden stretching off into the distance between two great rows of camellias.*

STRACHAN HOUSE

This handsomely porticoed home in the Garden District is the house where Jefferson Davis died. Ionic below and Corinthian above, the columns of this double gallery create an architectural effect familiar in the neighborhood, while indoors the woodwork and furnishings are notable, even for New Orleans.

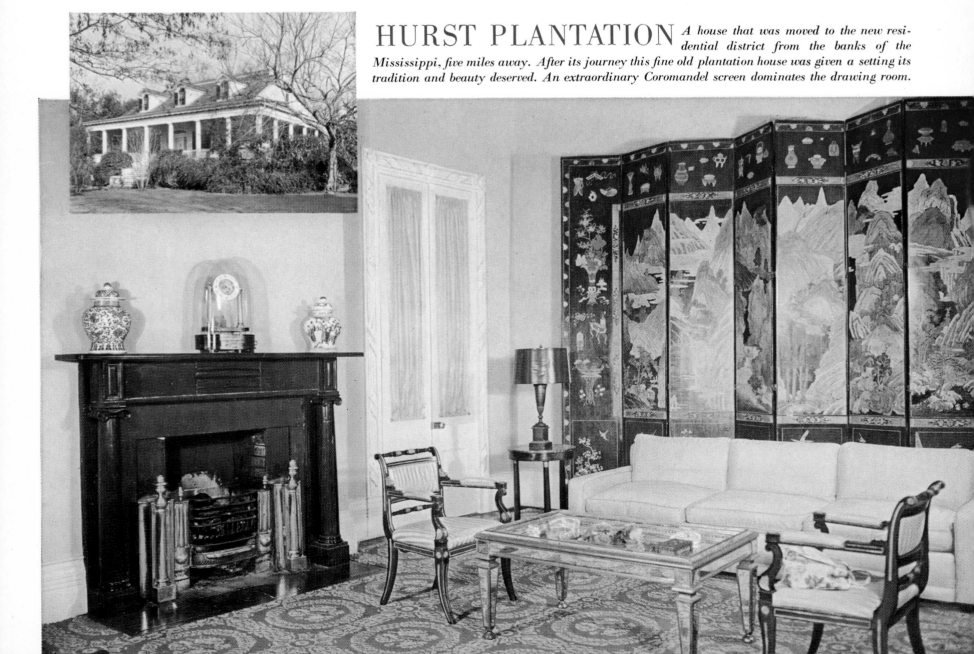

HURST PLANTATION
A house that was moved to the new residential district from the banks of the Mississippi, five miles away. After its journey this fine old plantation house was given a setting its tradition and beauty deserved. An extraordinary Coromandel screen dominates the drawing room.

THIS beautiful adobe church was built in the 1790's at near-by Carmel. The work was done by native Indian labor under the skillful direction of Manuel Estévan Ruiz, a master mason from Spain. The heavy tile roof held until 1852, when along with the fortunes of Monterey it collapsed—many of the tiles being taken to patch the roofs of that temporarily forsaken town. Now carefully restored, its patio splendidly gardened, it is the showpiece of the peninsula.

Monterey

Where Spain and New England combined in creating a style that has since spread all over the country

WINDING through the town of Monterey, there runs a continuous orange-yellow strip, painted down the center of certain streets like a traffic line; a slender golden track, with arrows urging you to follow the trail. If you do, you come in the course of your little trip to every old house of any distinction in the city; each house marked by an attractive plaque like the one for the De la Torre adobe at the bottom of this page. But because along the route each indicated house is in itself also marked by special qualities which alone are enough to capture the attention, the signs are simply footnotes to the story that unfolds as you trace out the line.

The story of the houses begins with the time when California was a colony of Spain, and Monterey the most important seaport on the coast. Timber was plentiful, but lumbermen and carpenters weren't; and besides, the Indians already had a building material that was better and easier by far. They merely molded blocks of mud from the ground, let them dry hard in the sun, and laid them up into walls—a trick that had worked its way up from Mexico, where adobe had been a building material for thousands of years. And with the simple plastered stone-walled houses of their native Mediterranean in mind, the Spaniards then had at hand a manner, as well as a method, of building which made a heavenly marriage in the climate of Monterey, creating a tradition which of course the Mexicans carried on when eventually they took over from the Spaniards.

In the meanwhile, as many of the Monterey houses make clear, Americans had been coming in, mostly from New England; and in the ships they sailed around Cape Horn, they carried not only certain architectural ideas from New England, but actual house parts too—doors, windows, moldings—along with Eastern carpenters who did their work the Eastern way. However, the basic form for Monterey houses had been established; adobe was ideal for the walls; the flat-pitched roofs with wide overhangs to shade the windows below were perfect for the climate; so these important characteristic features were retained. It is only in the woodwork that the houses tell their Eastern inheritance; but the blending of the two Colonials was such a happy one that the style created here has after a hundred years become the most popular in the country, next, of course, to the Cape Cod cottage—which, after all, was one of its forebears.

Some of the houses still show what happened to Monterey in the 1850's, shortly after California became part of the United States. Gold had been discovered—but just too far away. The town became deserted, and the houses for many years were left at the mercy of the weather. But there is a happy ending, as you can see, for practically all those which remain have been beautifully restored—and the others make most romantic ruins.

EXTERIOR PHOTOGRAPHS BY RICHARD PRATT

INTERIOR PHOTOGRAPHS BY HENRY FLANNERY

Once in the center of the city, the charming Casa Bonifacio has been reconstructed with its original adobe in the more congenial setting of an open residential section.

In the ancient but beautifully preserved customhouse, close to famous Fisherman's Wharf, ship arrivals in the old Spanish and Mexican days were celebrated with revels.

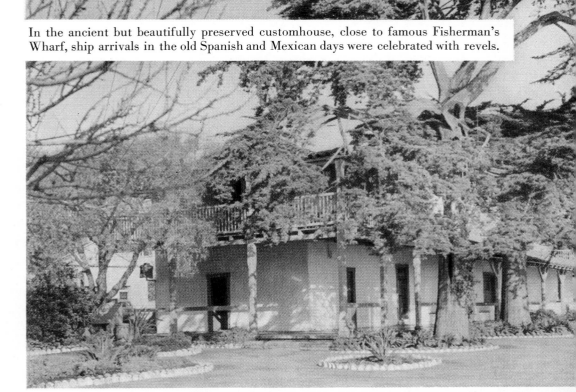

Half-hidden here under flowering trees, the De la Torre house, one of Monterey's most appealing adobes, was once sold, during the hard times, for $7.50 in back taxes.

A FEW years after he came to Monterey from Boston in 1832 and built this house, Thomas Oliver Larkin, who by then was already one of the first citizens of California, furthered a style which, in bringing together Eastern Colonial and Spanish Provincial, has become traditional with Monterey. Characteristic features: long horizontal lines, hip roof, porches.

DOMINATED by the huge, intricately carved teakwood Chinese bed, and further set with other Chinese pieces, paintings and accessories, the principal bedroom of the Larkin house shows the influence that is naturally reflected in a home so closely associated with trade between California and the Orient. Note the pioneer simplicity of the plank ceiling.

THE deep embrasured windows of the Larkin house dining room reveal the thickness of walls laid up of large sun-dried adobe bricks, plastered and whitewashed; while the furniture from early New England completes the picture of the life of the first wealthy settlers from the East who did so much to develop Monterey's now familiar architectural manner.

The
Larkin House

THE garden of the Casa Amesti, one of the loveliest adobes in Monterey, is a tribute to the taste of its present owner, the well-known decorator, Frances Elkins, who has not only restored the fine old house with great sensitivity but has embellished it inside and out in a manner that equips it most appropriately for contemporary living. The garden has a distinctly Mediterranean flavor, the formality of the clipped boxwood and columnar yews relieved by the softer forms of lemons and fig trees and palms.

The Amesti House

MRS. ELKINS' little blue library reflects, as it should, the personality of the present owner of the old Amesti house, just as the cool old thick-walled building itself still very much emanates its original atmosphere of simplicity. It was built in the 1830's by a rich ranchero of the region, Don José Amesti, who then a little later gave it to his daughter Carmen when she married Don Santiago (born James) McKinley, a former Scotch sailor who was left ashore off a whaler at San Francisco in the '20's and became a naturalized Mexican—which would indicate that the house has romantic memories along with its architectural charm.

BIBLIOGRAPHY

BENNETT, G. F.: *Early Architecture of Delaware*, Historical Press, Inc., Wilmington, 1932.

BRIGGS, M. S.: *The Homes of the Pilgrim Fathers in England and America*, Oxford University Press, New York, 1932.

COUSINS, F., and RILEY, P. M.: *The Colonial Architecture of Salem*, Little, Brown & Company, Boston, 1919.

DAVIS, DORSEY and HALL: *Alexandria Houses*, Architectural Book Publishing Company, Inc., New York, 1946.

EBERLEIN, H. D., and HUBBARD, C. V.: *Portrait of a Colonial City*, J. B. Lippincott Company, Philadelphia, 1939.

FORMAN, HENRY CHANDLEE: *Early Manor and Plantation Houses of Maryland*, Waverley Press, Baltimore, 1934.

FRARY, I. T.: *Thomas Jefferson, Architect and Builder*, Garrett & Massie, Inc., Richmond, 1931.

HAMLIN, TALBOT: *Greek Revival Architecture in America*, Oxford University Press, New York, 1944.

HANNAFORD, D. R., and EDWARDS, R.: *Spanish Colonial or Adobe Architecture of California*, Architectural Book Publishing Company, New York, 1931.

HIGGINS-WOOTEN: *New Castle, Delaware*, Houghton Mifflin Company, Boston, 1939.

HOWELLS, JOHN MEAD: *The Architectural Heritage of the Piscataqua*, Architectural Book Publishing Company, New York, 1937.

KELLY, J. FREDERICK: *The Early Domestic Architecture of Connecticut*, Yale University Press, New Haven, 1924.

KIMBALL, FISKE: *Domestic Architecture of the American Colonies and of the Early Republic*, Bobbs-Merrill Company, New York, 1928.

————: *Thomas Jefferson, Architect; Original Designs in the Collection of Thomas Jefferson Coolidge*, Riverside Press, Boston, 1916.

————: *Samuel McIntire, Carver, the Architect of Salem*, Southworth-Anthoensen Press, Portland, 1940.

MAJOR, HOWARD: *The Domestic Architecture of the Early American Republic: The Greek Revival*, J. B. Lippincott Company, Philadelphia, 1926.

RICCIUTI, ITALO W.: *New Orleans and its Environs*, William Helburn, Inc., New York, 1938.

STONEY, SAMUEL G.: *Plantations of the Carolina Low Country*, Carolina Art Association, Charleston, 1938.

WATERMAN, THOMAS T.: *The Mansions of Virginia*, University of North Carolina Press, Chapel Hill, 1945.

American Guide Series: Detailed guidebooks for all states represented in this book, prepared by the Federal Writers' Project of the Works Progress Administration between 1936 and 1941. Houghton Mifflin Company, Boston, and Oxford University Press, New York.

The White Pine Series of Architectural Monographs, Published by Russell F. Whitehead, Marchbanks Press, New York, 1918–1931 (out of print).

INDEX